A nostalgic look at

BELFAST
TROLLEYBUSES

1938-1968

Mike Maybin

Silver Link Publishing Ltd

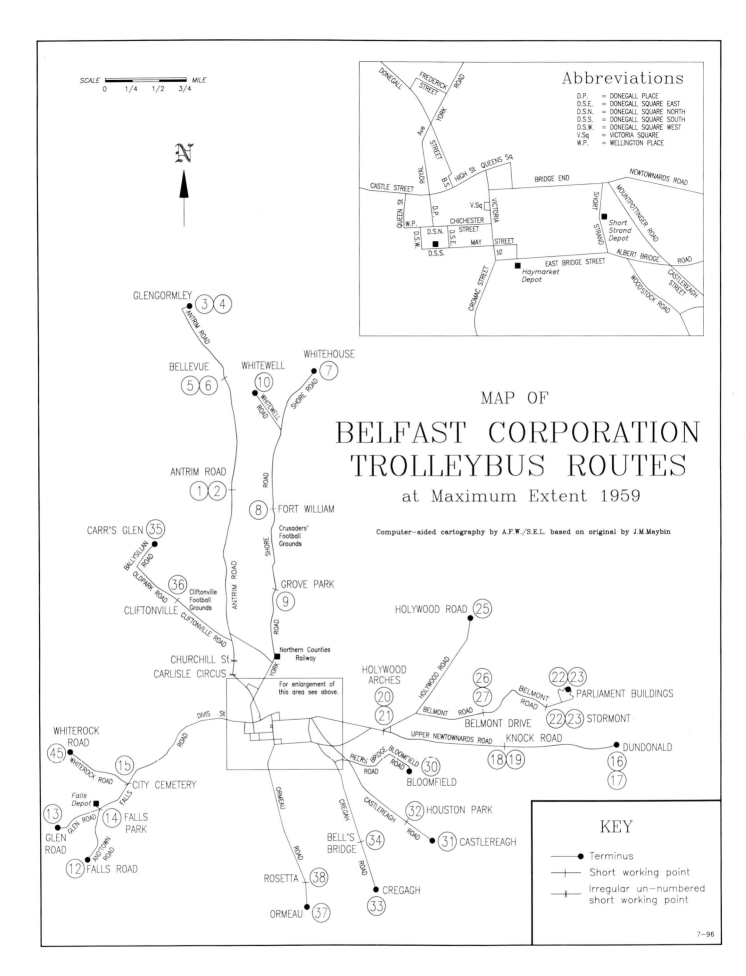

SCALE |■■■■■■■■■■| MILE
0   1/4   1/2   3/4

N

Abbreviations

D.P. = DONEGALL PLACE
D.S.E. = DONEGALL SQUARE EAST
D.S.N. = DONEGALL SQUARE NORTH
D.S.S. = DONEGALL SQUARE SOUTH
D.S.W. = DONEGALL SQUARE WEST
V.Sq = VICTORIA SQUARE
W.P. = WELLINGTON PLACE

DONEGALL STREET
FREDERICK STREET
ROYAL AVE
YORK STREET
B.S.
HIGH St
QUEENS Sq
BRIDGE END
NEWTOWNARDS ROAD
CASTLE STREET
QUEEN St
W.P.
D.P.
D.S.W.
D.S.N.
D.S.E.
V.Sq
CHICHESTER STREET
VICTORIA STREET
MAY STREET
SHORT STRAND
MOUNTPOTTINGER ROAD
Short Strand Depot
D.S.S.
CROMAC STREET
Haymarket Depot
EAST BRIDGE STREET
ALBERT BRIDGE ROAD
CASTLEREAGH STREET
WOODSTOCK ROAD

GLENGORMLEY ③④
ANTRIM ROAD

BELLEVUE ⑤⑥
WHITEWELL ⑩
WHITEWELL ROAD
SHORE ROAD
WHITEHOUSE ⑦

ANTRIM ROAD ①②
ROAD
⑧ FORT WILLIAM
SHORE ROAD
Crusaders' Football Grounds

CARR'S GLEN ㉟
BALLYSILLAN ROAD
OLDPARK ROAD
③⑥ Cliftonville Football Grounds
CLIFTONVILLE CLIFTONVILLE ROAD

MAP OF
BELFAST CORPORATION
TROLLEYBUS ROUTES
at Maximum Extent 1959

Computer–aided cartography by A.F.W./S.E.L. based on original by J.M.Maybin

GROVE PARK ⑨

HOLYWOOD ROAD ㉕

ANTRIM ROAD
ROAD

CHURCHILL St
CARLISLE CIRCUS
Northern Counties Railway
YORK ROAD

For enlargement of this area see above.

HOLYWOOD ARCHES
⑳㉑

HOLYWOOD ROAD
㉖㉗
BELMONT ROAD
㉒㉓ PARLIAMENT BUILDINGS
BELMONT ROAD
㉒㉓ STORMONT
BELMONT DRIVE

DIVIS St
ROAD

BECRS BRIDGE ROAD
BLOOMFIELD ROAD
UPPER NEWTOWNARDS ROAD
KNOCK ROAD
DUNDONALD

WHITEROCK ROAD ㊺
WHITEROCK ROAD
⑮
CITY CEMETERY

⑱⑲
㉚ BLOOMFIELD
⑯⑰

Falls Depot
FALLS ROAD
⑬ ⑭ FALLS PARK
GLEN ROAD
ORMEAU ROAD
CREGAGH ROAD
CASTLEREAGH ROAD
㉜ HOUSTON PARK

GLEN ROAD
⑫ FALLS ROAD
ANDTOWN ROAD
BELL'S BRIDGE
㉞
㉛ CASTLEREAGH

ROSETTA ㊳
CREGAGH ROAD
㉝ CREGAGH

ORMEAU ㊲

KEY

•——— Terminus
—|— Short working point
—✕— Irregular un–numbered short working point

7–96

CONTENTS

BIBLIOGRAPHY

Books and Reports

Bett, W. H. *The Theory of Fare Collection on Railways and Tramways* (Light Railway Transport League, 1943)

Blacker, K. *Trolleybus* (1975)
   Vintage Bus Annual No 1 (1979)

City of Belfast Ceremony to Commemorate the Termination of Trolleybus Operation (1968)

Jenkinson, K. *Preserved Buses* (1974)

Joyce, J., King, J. S. and Newman, A. G. *British Trolleybus Systems*

Joyce, J. *The Study of Passenger Transport in Britain* (1967)
   Trolleybus Trails (Ian Allan, 1963)

Kaye, D. *Buses and Trolleybuses 1919 to 1945* (1970)
   Buses and Trolleybuses since 1945 (1968)

Larmour, P. *An Illustrated Architectural Guide* (1987)

Maybin, Mike *A Nostalgic Look at Belfast Trams since 1945* (Silver Link Publishing Ltd, 1994)
   Belfast Corporation Tramways (LRTL, 1981)

Owen, N. *The History of British Trolleybuses* (1974)

Planning Proposals for the Belfast Area - Interim Report (Cmd 227, HMSO, 1945)

Pole, F. J. C. 'Transport Conditions in Northern Ireland' (Cmd 160, HMSO, 1934)

PSV Circle *NIRTB/UTA/Ulsterbus Fleet List* (1972)
   Belfast Corporation Fleet List (1968)

Symons, R. D. H. and Creswell, P. R. *British Trolleybuses* (1966)

Thompson, H. N. and McClintock, W. 'Public Transport in Northern Ireland' (Cmd 198, HMSO, 1938)

Ulster Architectural Heritage Society *Central Belfast* (1993)

Periodicals (various editions)

Belfast Corporation Transport Department Annual Reports
Belfast Corporation Transport Committee Minutes
Belfast Newsletter
Belfast Telegraph
Buses and *Buses Illustrated*
Irish News
Journal of the Transport Ticket Society
Modern Tramway
Northern Whig
Omnibus Magazine
Trolleybus Magazine
Ulster Year Book

© Mike Maybin 1996
Route maps © J. C. Gilham and Irwin Miller
General system map © Stan Letts and Arthur Whitehouse

First published in December 1996

British Library Cataloguing in Publication Data

A catalogue record for this book is available from the British Library.

ISBN 1 85794 068 7

Silver Link Publishing Ltd
Unit 5
Home Farm Close
Church Street
Wadenhoe
Peterborough PE8 5TE
Tel (01832) 720440
Fax (01832) 720531
e-mail: pete@slinkp-p.demon.co.uk

Printed and bound in Great Britain

ACKNOWLEDGEMENTS

I WOULD LIKE to acknowledge, with very great thanks, a number of people who have helped in one way or another in the production of this book. In particular the contributions of my wife Margaret and my children Andrew, James and Jenny, who allowed me the time to undertake the work rather than the husbandly and fatherly duties that they could have quite reasonably expected!

As with my earlier book on Belfast trams, David Harvey lent me his collection of Belfast photographs, of which there are over 600, and I thank him for his permission to use a number of them in the book. He also read and commented upon the text at the draft stage.

Richard Whitford also allowed me access to his photographic collection. Not only have I used a number of them, but also my original research was greatly helped by the availability of this organised and accurate archive. He also read and commented on the draft.

Billy Montgomery helped identify most of the private and commercial vehicles in the pictures, in addition to making available a number of photographs, while David Irwin read the draft and made a number of technical contributions.

Irwin Miller allowed me to 'tap into' his encyclopaedic knowledge of the Belfast trolleybus overhead line layout and contributed to the overhead layout maps, and John Gillham permitted me to use a number of his photographs and in addition drew the master from which the area maps were taken. Large copies of the master may be obtained from John at 209 Gunnersbury Park, Ealing, London W5. Stan Letts and Arthur Whitehouse produced the system map at the beginning of the book.

In addition I would like to thank each of the following people for their contribution to the book in one way or another:

Robin Adams; Roger Atkinson, Chester; Peter Bainbridge; Denis Battams, London; J. F. Barrett, Denton; George Beattie, Haverfordwest; Henry Beer, Belfast; Robert Beggs, formerly of Ulster Folk and Transport Museum; Ken Blacker, Lowestoft; Roy Brook, Huddersfield; Gary Burrows, Belfast; W. A. Camwell, Birmingham; C. Carter, London; Frank Clegg, Citybus, Belfast; Sam Clyde, Bangor; Des Coakham, Ballymoney; Paul Cresswell; R. J. Durrant, Orpington; Clifton Flewitt, Dublin; John Girvan, Bangor; Roy Golds, South Croydon; Mr Grant, Ballymena; John Gray, formerly of Belfast Central Library; Bob Gray, Belfast; George Green, Buckinghamshire; Edgar Griffith, Whiteabbey; Philip Groves, Nottinghamshire; Max Hale, Citybus; Gilbert Harkness, Belfast; Fred Harsh, Ballynahinch; George Hearse, Ramsey, IOM; E. M. H. Humphreys, Birmingham; Bob Hunter, Antrim; Bram Irvine, Belfast; R. C. Jackson, Worsley; D. A. Jones, London; D. W. K. Jones, Reigate; Jim Joyce, London; Fred Kelso, Newtownabbey; Terry King, Woking; Reg Ludgate, Belfast; Robert Mack, Leeds; Nan Maybin, Bangor; Arthur Muskett, Belfast; Peter McBride, Bangor; Eric McDevitte, Ballyclare; Jimmy McFarlane, Belfast; Eddie McIlwaine, *Belfast Telegraph*; John McKegney, Armagh; Robert O'Sullivan, Christchurch; Mrs D. Parr, Bingley; John Price, Peterborough; H. B. Priestley, Mansfield; John Priestley, Bedford; A. Ratcliffe, West Sussex; Leila Rea, Bangor; John Reeves, Bognor Regis; Mike Russell, Swindon; John Saunders, Belfast; R. H. G. Simpson, Oxford; Cecil Slator, Belfast; J. H. Smith, Belfast; Fred Stone, Carrickfergus; Philip Stoy, Exmouth; J. N. Symons, Stoke-on-Trent; Robin Symons, Berkshire; H. Taylor, Edgware; Brian Walter, Hounslow; John Whitehead, Reading; Peter Williams, West Sussex; Charles Wilson, Belfast; and Richard Wiseman, Mansfield.

A number of photographs credited to R. F. Mack have been used with the agreement of the National Trolleybus Association, who currently hold the copyright.

The staffs of the following bodies deserve my appreciation and thanks for their help, often going much further than their official duties required:

Belfast Central Library; Citybus, Belfast; Control Systems, Uxbridge; Linenhall Library, Belfast; Park Royal Ltd; Public Record Office for Northern Ireland, Belfast; Ulster Folk and Transport Museum, Cultra; and Ulster Museum, Belfast.

FOREWORD

Mary Peters CBE

ALTHOUGH I was born in Halewood, in Lancashire, I moved to Northern Ireland when I was 11. This was because my father was promoted to manager by the Liverpool Victoria Friendly Society, and not as a result of any great desire on my part to do so. Indeed, I found the North Antrim accent so difficult to follow at school in Ballymena that I needed an interpreter in my first few days! However, this feeling of strangeness soon wore off and I settled in at my new school and home quite easily.

My father was promoted again and our family moved to Portadown. My brother and I attended Portadown College, where we both threw ourselves into all the sporting (and other) activities that the school provided. I greatly enjoyed the schoolgirl athletics events and the occasional forays to 'the mainland' to take part in national competitions. However, as a young woman I realised that it would be wise to obtain some qualifications with which to earn a living. (At that time I had not seriously thought of my talent at athletics as being a base for a full-time career.) I had developed an interest in teaching - and I believe some skill at sewing and cooking - which resulted in my going to the Belfast College of Domestic Science.

Initially I shared 'digs' with a school friend, at North Parade on the Ormeau Road, and my journey to College each morning was by trolleybus. I had the choice of taking a trolley down Ormeau Road and Cromac Street or a petrol bus, which went by Botanic Avenue. (Of course I know they actually ran on diesel oil, but everybody in Belfast called them 'petrol buses'.)

I have fond recollections of the Belfast trolleybuses; whether this is because of the mostly happy associations of college life I am not sure. My memories of trolleybuses are of their silence, their bulk and their reliability. They also seemed much more frequent than today's Citybuses and I don't recollect many long waits at bus stops.

By the time I was old enough to use the trolleybuses on my own they were red, but I have a vague memory of a family visit to Belfast as a child and seeing blue trolleybuses. Certainly the insides of some vehicles had blue leather seats until the early 1960s. I also remember that the older vehicles had wind-up clocks downstairs, which kept remarkably good time.

I later moved to Willowbank Gardens, which links the Cavehill Road with the Antrim Road. Again I used to catch the trolleybus to College. It left from the end of the road, and as it happened there was a choice of two trolleybus routes into town. One was via Duncairn Gardens and York Street, while the other passed Carlisle Circus

and went down Clifton Street. This was lucky for me as the two routes together gave a 5-minutes service.

The Carlisle Circus route always seemed a bit illogical to me. Instead of the trolleybus going straight down Donegall Street and turning right into Royal Avenue, which was the direct way, it turned left into North Queen Street and almost immediately right into Frederick Street. It then turned right again at the bottom into York Street. Why they did this I could never understand, since neither the trams nor the petrol buses seemed to need to do so.

I remember one occasion when the driver forgot to make the left turn at North Queen Street, and suddenly the bus slowed to a crawl as the trolleys left the overhead wires and bounced about wildly in the air. The driver had to explain to his passengers why they were stranded in the middle of Upper Donegall Street, while the queue of traffic that had formed up behind was becoming increasingly impatient and expressing it in the

traditional way! To his evident embarrassment the driver told the conductor to phone for the breakdown wagon and told the passengers that it would be a little while before help arrived.

After qualifying I taught for a while at Graymount Secondary School, which was near the Shore Road end of Gray's Lane. At that time I was furiously practising my shot-putting. On those days when I was not working with the girls at after-school activities, I took the trolleybus from Gray's Lane to Castle Junction and got a petrol bus to Ormeau Park, where I trained. Usually I carried my shot in a paper bag, and on one occasion I was travelling upstairs when the conductor demanded that I put it in the luggage compartment under the stairs according to the regulations. I was rather surprised, never having been asked before (or since). Rather than have it roll about the bus, I said I should prefer to keep it with me. The conductor became quite officious and demanded that either the parcel went in the luggage compartment or we both could walk. Anxious not to waste precious training time, I reluctantly handed over my brown paper parcel containing my 8 lb 13 oz shot! (For those of you who are more familiar with metric measurements, that is about 4 kg.)

Not expecting such a dead weight from such a small parcel, the conductor dropped it on the floor. The shot rolled to the back, down the stairs with a clatter that can be better imagined than described, on to the platform, through the open doorway and off the trolleybus! Of course the bus had to stop while I retrieved the shot, and the conductor was somewhat less than popular with the rest of the passengers.

One regular event that I don't think happened in other cities was the paper boys getting on the trolleybuses at Castle Junction from around 4 o'clock to sell the *Belfast Telegraph* to tired homeward-bound workers. The boys seemed to ride free of charge, but obviously provided a very useful and welcome service. When they had 'worked the bus' they got off and boarded the next one. One young man, whom I had seen earlier at teaching practice, and who had experienced considerable difficulty with theoretical mathematics, appeared to be able to cope with the practical arithmetic associated with change giving with great expertise!

I think my final memory of Belfast's trolleybuses was of the cat's cradle of wires that was put up, I think in the late 1950s, around the City Hall. I am sure that they were all necessary for the efficient working of the system, but there did seem to be an awful lot of them. When I later travelled through European cities, many of which had still their trolleybuses, I don't ever remember any of them having as many overhead wires as Belfast.

Although I am not a native-born Ulsterwoman, I have come to look on Northern Ireland as my home and on Belfast as my city. I am delighted therefore to contribute a little of my happy memories (or at least those associated with trolleybuses) to this book. Belfast trolleybuses were around during my teenage and early adult years and inevitably were associated with a very important part of my life. I remember them with great affection.

THE BELFAST trolleybus system grew to be the largest provincial fleet in the British Isles, with a maximum of 245 vehicles - only London had more. However, it is now almost 30 years since trolleybuses glided along Belfast's streets, and an entire generation of people has grown up without having been able to experience them. It is appropriate, therefore, to give a short summary of how they worked, and indeed how they differed from trams.

How trolleybuses work

In many ways trolleybuses were always regarded as a hybrid form of transport, combining some of the characteristics of both trams and buses. Like trams they depended upon electricity for their power, but like buses could pull into the kerb. Like trams they were dependent on the fixed overhead line equipment, but physically they looked more like buses. However, the legislation under which they functioned was in most cases quite different from that which governed bus operation; for example, they did not require to pass any form of PSV test.

Trolleybuses were powered by electricity generated centrally and supplied to the vehicles by overhead wires erected along the line of route. Being rubber-tyred vehicles they required a second overhead wire for the return current (trams used the steel rails for their return). There were only two foot-pedals, one for power and the other for braking. All 'native' Belfast trolleybus power pedals were to the left, while the brake pedal was on the right, but the 'Wolverhamptons' (sometimes known as 'Wanderers') had theirs the other way round, and there were a few near misses in the depot before they were modified! There was also a hand-brake for parking. Most Belfast trolleybuses carried traction batteries, which meant that they could move slowly under their own power for very short distances. The exceptions were the semi-utilities (131 to 142) and the former Wolverhampton vehicles (235 to 245). Perhaps surprisingly, the full utility vehicles (129 and 130) carried a set of traction batteries.

Initially the trolley booms required considerable strength to lower the trolleyheads from the wires, but the fitting of 'anti-attrition' heads later considerably reduced the effort needed and made life much easier for slightly built conductors. The graphite grease used to lubricate the trolley wires, when mixed with the brass of the heads, produced a dark green stain on the rear panel. In later years this was disguised by painting the panel khaki.

The overhead wires

Belfast's overhead wiring facilities around the City Hall after the one-way scheme was introduced in 1958 gave the city's trolleybuses as much flexibility of movement as motorbuses. The complexity of wiring necessary to achieve this was, I believe, unequalled in the world's trolleybus systems.

Almost every route had its boarding stop (and overhead 'siding'), which meant that buses could pull in from the 'main line' to allow passengers to board without holding up vehicles behind. However, unlike trams, trolleybuses were 'single-ended' vehicles and required to be turned at the terminus, and in the early days in Belfast reversers were installed in the overhead wiring to facilitate this manoeuvre. The first of these was erected at Fruithill Park on the Falls Road, and it was unusual in that it was installed on the right-hand side of the main road; for safety and traffic reasons, reversers were much more often installed on the left. The trolleybus drew up a sufficient distance past Fruithill Park to allow the trolleys to clear the 'frogs' in the overhead wiring - a white line was painted on the roadway to help the driver judge where to stop.

The 'frog' was the piece of overhead equipment that allowed the trolleys to follow a particular route. When the trolleybus reversed the trolley heads were guided into the minor road until they passed another set of sprung frogs. As the bus moved forward the trolleys were again guided in the required direction, this time turning left into the main road. There were four types of frogs in Belfast. 'Trailing' frogs were erected where two routes converged, and were simply brass castings designed in such a way that the trolley heads could approach the 'main line' from either of two directions; they operated without help from the platform crews. The other three types were known as 'facing frogs' for diverging routes. The choice of which type to use was dictated either by the frequency of service or, occasionally, by the awkwardness of the location.

For lightly trafficked routes, manual frogs were used: the spring-loaded mechanism was connected to a handle by a series of wires and pulleys and the handle itself attached to a convenient traction pole. Trolleybuses using the busier route simply drove through, while those bound for the secondary route stopped to allow the conductor to alight and operate the frog. He did so by pulling the handle down and holding it until the trolleys had been safely diverted; the legend used on the poles was 'PULL AND HOLD'. For busier services, 'reset' frogs were used. Buses on the primary route again simply coasted through, but when the conductor on a bus taking the secondary route operated the handle it locked the frog in position. He could then rejoin the bus and the trolleys themselves reset the frog for the primary route as they passed. The legend on these traction poles read 'PULL AND LET GO'.

Finally, for routes on which there was a frequent service even on the secondary road, automatic frogs were used. Again trolleybus drivers destined for the primary route took no action, but those making for the secondary route operated the frog electrically by increasing the power while the trolley heads were passing under a 'skate' in the negative wire in the overhead, at the same time applying a degree of hand-brake. This surge of electric current operated a solenoid, which in turn operated the frog. The trolley heads reset the frog as they passed through. Automatic frogs were also equipped with emergency handles, and the poles were also marked 'PULL AND LET GO'. In general, routes to the left required frogs to be operated, while those to the right did not.

Memories

Hugh McVeigh worked on the trolleybuses from 1942 to 1962 and during that period accumulated many anecdotes.

When Castlereagh was first converted to trolleybus operation in 1941, the route was extended from the tram terminus at the City Boundary to the Hillfoot Road, better known today as the Knock dual carriageway. During the war the blackout regulations were strictly enforced, which made turning very difficult. Both the Hillfoot and Castlereagh Roads were then very narrow, and the standard turning manoeuvre was to drive the vehicle forward across the Hillfoot Road and reverse to the left. The vehicle was then positioned to turn right and regain the Castlereagh Road. Without any light at all, the reverse turn in the direction of oncoming traffic was difficult and dangerous, and conductors usually helped their drivers with a discreetly shaded torch beam.

One night during this manoeuvre the conductor spotted a courting couple in the hedgerow who were far too preoccupied to notice. Much too considerate to make any comment, the conductor loudly gave the following advice to the driver: 'Back a bit. Back a bit more. Steady. Straighten up. A little more to me. Gently does it. Hold it. That's fine. Away you go when you're ready.'

There was a conductor who had the rare distinction of having an overhead frog named after him. John McDowell, who worked out of the Haymarket depot, spent most of his time on the Dundonald service, which joined the Stormont route at the Holywood Arches. On the into-town side there was originally a siding at the Connswater bridge, installed to allow trolleybuses to get back in sequence before going on to the City Centre. McDowell often managed to persuade his driver to pull into this siding until the next trolleybus from Stormont came along, then when it had loaded up McDowell's trolleybus would emerge from the siding and follow the Stormont vehicle into town. McDowell, of course, had to collect no more fares the whole way back to Castle Junction.

After some time other crews became fed up with this practice and took to referring to the frog as 'McDowell's switch'. Even this did not perturb the offender, and the problem was not resolved until one morning during the rush-hour a Stormont man, noticing McDowell's bus in the siding as usual, also got his conductor to pull the switch. The next Dundonald bus also went into the siding and the junction at Holywood Arches became blocked. Eventually McDowell's driver had no option but to pull out and go ahead. McDowell not only had to take a full trolleybus to the 'Junction', but had to put up with the constant complaints at every bus stop along the route from passengers frustrated by the delay in service.

Hugh's memory of the breakdown service is that it was very efficient. When petrol was in short supply and a trolleybus got a puncture, the usual practice was to send out a spare wheel in another trolleybus, which would be handed over to the crew. The passengers then changed vehicles and continued their journey. The breakdown gang changed the wheel and returned the original vehicle to the depot. Punctures were generally a welcome break in the monotony (unless they happened at the end of a shift), and on one occasion when the emergency call came through to the duty room at the depot, the caller 'forgot' to give his name and location. However, the engineer on duty recognised the voice and quickly ascertained the vehicle and route from the duty board. Although there was no way of knowing exactly where on the Antrim Road the bus was, the breakdown gang took the spare trolleybus to Castle Place and followed the route by way of Carlisle Circus to Glengormley. As there was no sign of the disabled trolleybus they concluded that it must be somewhere on the Duncairn Gardens part of the route, and returned to town that way. Still no sign, so another attempt was made to locate the vehicle. On the third trip tempers were becoming short, until someone spotted the offending bus parked as far down the reverser in Churchill Street as the overhead wiring would allow. The excuse offered by the driver and conductor was that they thought it a good idea to take the vehicle off the main road! (A photograph of this reverser appears in the North Belfast section.)

David Irwin, whose duty as an electrician in Falls Depot often required him to go out on breakdown work, remembers the occasion when he and Ted Thomas drove a replacement trolleybus to Parliament Buildings. A trolleybus had overshot the wires at Carson's statue in the middle of the Stormont estate and was headed towards the Upper Newtownards Road via the main processional entrance known as Prince of Wales Avenue. After the passengers had been transferred on to the other vehicle, David and Ted quickly realised that the stricken bus had insufficient battery power to take it back up the hill. They reckoned that the most effective solution was to free-wheel down Prince of Wales Avenue and hope that there would be sufficient momentum to carry them as far as the wires on the Upper Newtownards Road. Although the bus stopped a few yards short of the main road, enough passengers were willing to push!

The Dundonald turning circle was very tight. It involved an anticlockwise turn in the mouth of the junction of the Upper Newtownards and Comber Roads. To negotiate it safely the driver had to cross the into-town traffic from Newtownards and take the right fork in the direction of Comber. He was then required to swing across the centre line of the road to make a sharp left-hand turn in front of the Elk Inn public house. This was necessary so as to be correctly positioned to make another very sharp left turn back into the Upper Newtownards Road. As the second left turn was near a blind corner this was very tricky indeed. One driver recalled the morning he was stopped by a police officer who was intending to report him for careless driving, having crossed the centre line of the road by a considerable amount. The driver agreed that this was indeed the case, but pointed out that the manoeuvre would otherwise be impossible. The police officer disputed this and the exasperated driver challenged him to try it for himself. The challenge was accepted and on the next journey the driver stopped the bus short of the terminus and handed over the wheel. The police officer crossed the traffic and entered the Comber Road without incident and, keeping well to the correct side of the centre line turned left at the Elk Inn. There was then the sound of crunching metal as the side of the trolleybus caught the pedal of the policeman's bicycle and pulled it under the bus. There was a great deal of embarrassment to the policeman and much amusement for the bus crew and passengers! (There is an early photograph of Dundonald turning circle in the East Belfast section.)

Probably the most unusual tribute paid to the speed and silence of the Belfast trolleybus was that by a girl whose main activity was the provision of home comforts to lonely GIs during the war. In reply to a friend, she said, 'Trolleybuses? Oh they're just like them Yanks - they creep up in the dark behind you and are on top of you before you know where you are.'

Gary Burrows remembers the occasion when he was a passenger on the Dundonald route and the bus had filled with passengers. Several times the conductor asked his passengers to 'move on up the car, please', but received no response. Finally on the third time of asking and being again ignored, he lost patience and shouted, 'Please move further up the car - the rear end is going to the same place as the front'! The passengers doubled up with laughter and complied.

Liveries

The first trolleybuses (fleet numbers 1-14) were delivered in a blue and white livery in the streamlined style fashionable in the pre-war years. The off-white or cream sometimes attributed to Belfast trams and trolleybuses actually resulted from a combination of weathering and several coats of varnish. The main side and rear panels were lined out in gold and the words 'BELFAST CORPORATION' appeared in shaded letters beneath the lower deck windows. A large transfer of the city's coat-of-arms was placed near the centre of the lower side panels and a smaller version appeared on the front of the vehicle. The arms carried the motto 'PRO TANTO QUID RETRIBUAMUS', a rough translation of which is 'For so much what shall we return?' Shaded gold fleet numbers (preceded by a 'T') were provided at the front, back and both sides. Several of the original fleet were supplied with the entire front of the vehicle painted white, but the standard batch of AECs (fleet number 15 onwards) had a blue front to waist level, and the gold lining was omitted because of wartime austerity.

As the blackout regulations came onto force, mudguard edges were painted white and a white band was applied near ground level, vaguely giving the appearance of bumpers! The route number and 'via' screens were blacked out to save linen and the headlights were heavily masked.

Shortly after the war it was felt that blue paint was less durable than red, so a bus and a trolleybus were painted red and presented to the Council at the City Hall. The new livery was duly adopted and over the next couple of years applied to the entire fleet of buses and trolleybuses; the colour of the trams was, however, not changed. The last trolleybus in the old blue livery was 45 (FZ 7830).

As an economy measure, the Transport Committee decided in September 1953 to omit the words 'BELFAST CORPORATION' from the sides of vehicles. Personally I think that the trolleybuses looked more attractive with the legend in place.

It is generally agreed that Belfast trolleybuses were well maintained both mechanically and in presentation. On more than one occasion Robin Adams, Belfast's last General Manager, had been known to order a vehicle back to the depot because it looked rather scruffy.

Mary Peters

I was delighted when Mary Peters agreed to write the Foreword. Although she was born in Lancashire, Mary's family moved to Ballymena in 1950 when her father received promotion. She attended Portadown College and Belfast College of Domestic Science, later teaching for a period in Graymount Girls' Secondary School.

However, it is for her athletic achievements that she is best known. She started competing in the pentathlon in 1956 and represented Great Britain in the 1964 Olympics, coming fourth in that event. Four years later in Mexico she finished ninth. In Munich in 1972 she came first, achieving not only a personal best, but a world record and an Olympic Gold Medal. This was the first Gold won by a Northern Ireland competitor, and Mary's achievement was the best possible antidote to the province's worst year for terrorist violence.

Edward Heath was Prime Minister at the time and Mary was invited to a reception to mark her success. Always quick to recognise the contribution of others, she invited her coach to the party. One of the Prime Minister's aides warned that the invitation was for 'competitors only', but Mary was not prepared to exclude her coach so declined the invitation.

Throughout the 1970s and early '80s Mary continued to compete in, and later to manage, international athletics at the highest level, including the British teams at the Moscow Olympics in 1980 and Los Angeles in 1984. She also received a number of awards during this period, including BBC Sports Personality (1972), Athletic Writers (1972) and Sports Writers (1972). In 1974 she received an honorary Doctorate of Science from The New University of Ulster and published her autobiography, *Mary P.* She was awarded an MBE in 1972 and became a CBE in 1990.

During the 1970s Mary campaigned long and hard for better athletics facilities for the children of Belfast, and in 1976 she opened the 'Mary Peters Track' in the south of the city. The following year she opened what has become a successful and flourishing business known as Mary Peters Sports Ltd.

However, there is a side of Mary that may not be so well known - except perhaps to those people directly involved. She gives a great deal of her time to a wide variety of important work for the benefit of the community. Although much of it is sport-related, such as membership of the National and Northern Ireland Sports Councils and trusteeship of the Sports Trust, Mary is or has also been involved with, for example, the Churchill Foundation Fellowship, the Northern Ireland Association of Youth Clubs, Riding for the Disabled, the BBC Broadcasting Council, the Friends of the Royal Victoria Hospital, and the Northern Ireland Tourist Board, to name but a few.

When she did eventually meet Prime Minister Heath, he asked which country she had represented in the recent Commonwealth Games. Mary replied, 'Northern Ireland, and I hope that you are as proud to be British as I am!' This remark was widely reported, and Mary's popularity knew no bounds. She became, and has remained, an honorary Ulsterwoman.

A BRIEF HISTORY OF BELFAST TROLLEYBUSES

THE BELFAST Corporation Act (NI) 1930 contained the legal authority for the operation of trolleybuses in Belfast. During the late 1920s the Corporation Tramways & Motors Committee had become increasingly concerned about several aspects of tramway operation in the city. First, large sections of tramway track, particularly in East Belfast, were approaching the end of their useful life. Second, the Department was well aware of the 'bad press' Belfast trams had received, unlike the buses, which were portrayed as modern, fast and comfortable. Third, morale in the Department was low - 1928 was the year of the 'Bus War', and finished with a public inquiry. The resulting report was critical of departmental management and the replacement of Samuel Carlisle as General Manager was inevitable. He was succeeded by William Chamberlain of Leeds.

Nevertheless, considerable capital was invested in the generating plant and feeder equipment for the trams and the Corporation was reluctant to abandon them regardless of their useful life. On the UK mainland trolleybuses were seen as the best of both worlds. They could be as modern, fast and comfortable as motor buses, with the additional advantage of continuing to use the generating plant and equipment.

With an eye to the future, therefore, the 1930 Act incorporated the power to operate trolleybuses. Interestingly the area for which the power was given was the City of Belfast, including any road outside the city on which the Corporation was empowered to operate trams, and any other road outside the city for the purpose of providing a turning circle or gaining access to depots. Permission from the Ministry of Home Affairs was, however, required. Nevertheless, the Corporation was specifically prohibited from manufacturing any trolleybus parts other than bodies. Section 7 of the Act exempted trolleybuses from the Motor Vehicles (Traffic and Regulation) Act (NI) 1926, while Section 10 defined the new trolley vehicle undertaking as part of the tramways. Taken together, these two sections had the effect of trolleybus drivers not requiring to have driving licences.

Nothing was done for several years, as the tramway system (and new bus undertaking) had settled down to a period of financial and operational stability. Major McCreary, the Permanent Way Engineer, became General Manager after Chamberlain returned to England to chair the newly formed North Western Traffic Commissioners. In 1936 McCreary brought forward a report to the Tramways Committee indicating that if the price of electricity remained 'at the most favourable tariff possible, then trolleybuses should be introduced as being the most suitable mode of transport to replace tramcars'. The track in Mountpottinger Road and the outer section of the Cregagh route, from Bell's Bridge to the terminus, was by then in a poor state and McCreary took the opportunity to replace trams with motor buses on both these sections. He shrewdly introduced protective fares on those sections of bus route that paralleled the trams and ensured that the trams continued to operate at a higher frequency. The next meeting of the Tramways Committee following these changes was held on Tuesday 6 October 1936, and McCreary presented his proposals to introduce an experimental trolleybus service. He chose the Falls Road route and gave the following reasons for nominating it: 'It is the tramcar route which is "least tied up" with other routes; it is of sufficient length to give a reasonable test to the new vehicles; there is on the route a depot, in which by withdrawing tramcars, space is available for trolleybuses; the track on the outer section between City Cemetery and the terminus is worn out and a decision at an early date will have to be made as to the policy for this route; and it lends itself at the City Centre to easy trolleybus operation - inwards by Queen Street, Wellington Place and Donegall Place and thence outwards by Castle Street.'

The term 'inwards' when used by the Tramways Department always referred inwards to Castle Junction, and, by extension, 'outwards' meant outwards from Castle Junction, which was regarded as the centre of the system.

There was one other reason for choosing Falls Road as the first trolleybus route. For almost its entire length it served a very densely populated area with a low rate of car ownership. Therefore considerable use of public transport could be guaranteed and the financial success of the scheme assured. The scheme was accepted by the Committee and later ratified by the City Council, paving the way for the introduction of Ireland's first (and only) trolleybus undertaking.

The vehicles

The vehicles were supplied on an unusual basis. Eight of the largest chassis manufacturers in the UK were asked whether they would be willing to lend vehicles for the duration of the experiment. Only one, Ransomes, Simms & Jeffries Ltd of Ipswich, declined. The other seven, Associated Equipment Company (AEC), Leyland, Guy, Sunbeam, Daimler, Crossley and Karrier each agreed to lend two vehicles on the understanding that they could be returned in the event of the Corporation not continuing with trolleybus operation.

The Department pursued the same policy of diversity in buying electrical equipment and bodies from various suppliers. The former were bought from Metropolitan-Vickers (Metro-Vick), English Electric (EEC), British Thompson-Houston (BTH), Crompton Parkinson, and Electrical Construction, while bodywork was provided by Harkness Coachworks of Belfast, Leyland, Cowieson of Glasgow, Crossley and Park Royal. This 'mixed bag' approach had the advantage of allowing the Corporation to assess each chassis, body and set of electrical equipment separately as well as in various combinations. For the precise combination in which the trolleybuses were assembled, please see the section on 'Fleet Summary'.

The overhead line equipment

The contract for the overhead line equipment was awarded to Clough Smith & Co Ltd. This was one of the foremost UK companies specialising in this work and the 'on-site' operation was supervised by the company's construction engineer, Mr A. Ratcliffe. For economy, McCreary chose to use as many of the existing tramway traction poles as possible, and the gantry system of overhead line support was adopted for the Falls Road route. This consisted of a steel tube of 2⅜ inch diameter clamped rigidly to opposite pairs of traction poles and supported by struts from the top of the poles to various points along the tube. Attached to the tubes, or cross-bars, were insulators, and 'ears' to which the trolley wire itself was clamped. The underside of the wire presented a smooth surface to the trolley heads.

The experimental route

The route was from Castle Junction ('outward' stop in Castle Street) by way of Castle Street, Divis Street, Falls Road and Andersonstown Road to the terminus at Fruithill Park. Intermediate turning circles were provided at City Cemetery (junction of Falls Road with Whiterock Road) and Falls Park (junction of Falls Road with Glen Road). This turning circle was opposite Falls Road Depot. Entry to both turning circles was achieved by manually operated frogs.

In tram days the normal weekday service from Castle Junction to City Cemetery was half-hourly until 7.30 am,

increasing to 5 minutes from City Centre to terminus. The replacement trolleybuses gave the same early morning service, with a 6-minutes service from Castle Junction to Fruithill Park, supplemented by a further 6-minute service from Castle Junction to City Cemetery at peak times. A maximum of 12 trolleybuses was required for the peak-time services. The fares remained at the same level and the preferential workmen's fares continued to be offered on the new vehicles.

The opening ceremony took place on 28 March 1938. The Lord Mayor, Sir Crawford McCullough, drove the last tram from Castle Street to Queen Street and the first trolleybus from there to Falls Park, where the depot manager, Patrick Graham, was complimented on the superb presentation of the new vehicles.

The new trolleybuses were an almost instantaneous success, although McCreary had been careful to make sure that the experiment took place in the most favourable circumstances. The Corporation Tramways & Motors Committee changed its name to Transport Committee with effect from 1 March 1938. McCreary presented his report 'Transport Policy' to the Transport Committee on 16 December of that year, and indicated that the new trolleybuses had caused no increase in traffic congestion in the main streets of the city centre.

On customer reaction, McCreary highlighted the fact that traffic receipts from trolleybuses had averaged 7 per cent more than those from tramcars, with no increase in fares. He recommended that the tramway system be abandoned and replaced with trolleybuses, and this recommendation was accepted by the City Council on 9 January 1939. The order of conversion was later decided as East Belfast, followed by the Southern routes and finishing with North Belfast. The Department ordered 114 AEC trolleybuses with electrical equipment by GEC and Harkness 68-seater bodywork.

Wartime

The declaration of war on 3 September 1939 had three immediate effects on public transport in Belfast. The first was that McCreary immediately left for the War Office to report for duty. He was succeeded by Samuel Carlisle (former General Manager), who was appointed Acting General Manager for the duration, with Joseph Mackle as his deputy. The second was the introduction of petrol rationing and the consequent immediate reduction in petrol bus services. From 25 September 1939 only those bus routes not duplicating a tram service remained, and finally the order for 114 trolleybuses was summarily cut to 88 by the Ministry of War Transport. Indeed, Belfast was one of the very few cities in the UK to be allowed any new trolleybuses with non-utility bodies at all.

In response to the fear of a German invasion all kinds of direction information was removed, which initially included destination information on trams and buses. Intended to confuse enemy paratroopers, it certainly succeeded in confusing the Belfast travelling public!

The erection of the overhead line equipment in preparation for the conversion of the East Belfast routes began in 1940. The original scheme included the Cregagh, Castlereagh, Dundonald, Stormont, Bloomfield and

Ormeau via Cromac Street routes (Ormeau via Botanic Avenue was seen as part of the South Belfast scheme). The intention was to operate Cregagh and Bloomfield via Albert Bridge only, Castlereagh via Queen's Bridge only, and Dundonald and Stormont via both Bridges alternately. This would replicate the pattern of tramcar services.

The plan was to operate all the East Belfast trolleybuses inward to Castle Junction by way of Victoria Street, High Street and Castle Place, and outward through Donegall Place and Chichester Street. The Cregagh route was opened on 13 February 1941 and served Chichester Street, Victoria Street, East Bridge Street, Albert Bridge, Woodstock Road and Cregagh Road, with a reverser terminus at Cregagh Park. Similar to the design of the reverser at Fruithill Park on the Falls Road, trolleybuses pulled up on the left-hand side of the road just past Cregagh Park and, with the help of the conductor, reversed into the Park; when they were ready to depart for the City they turned right out on to the Cregagh Road. An intermediate terminus was also installed at Bell's Bridge, and trolleybuses reversed into Graham Gardens to turn. In July 1951 the terminus was improved by erecting a loop on land near Cregagh Park, while the road layout at Bell's Bridge was altered, probably in the early 1960s, and trolleybuses turned at the new roundabout.

The next route to open was Castlereagh on 5 June 1941. From Castle Junction the trolleybuses operated via Donegall Place and Chichester Street, turning left into Victoria Street, then by way of Ann Street, Queen's Bridge, Bridge End, Mountpottinger Road, Castlereagh Street and Castlereagh Road. A reverser was installed at the junction of Knockbreda Road and Castlereagh Road, and trolleybuses crossed the Hillfoot Road (as that part of Knock Road was then known) into Ballygowan Road and reversed left into the Hillfoot Road, before turning right into Castlereagh Road for the return journey into town. A reverser was established at Houston Park, which became the intermediate terminus for Castlereagh. In the 1950s the reverser at Knockbreda Road was replaced by a loop built in the mouth of the junction, and around 1961 this was replaced by a specially built 'off-road' terminal loop about 100 yards short of the junction on the 'into-town' side of the road.

Most of the overhead wiring had been constructed at the same time, and the rate at which routes were opened was governed mainly by the rate at which new trolleybuses could be delivered.

One effect of the war was to increase passenger traffic dramatically. For example, the number of passengers carried by all three modes of transport in the year ended 31 March 1938 was 134,469,737, while by 1943 the figure had risen to 217,504,676 - a rise of over 60 per cent. The total number of vehicles available rose from 428 to 522 over the same period, an increase of less than 22 per cent. The effect of these trends was to increase significantly the average number of passengers per vehicle, and as each tram route was converted to trolleybus operation the trams were not withdrawn but re-allocated to other tram routes to increase carrying capacity.

The next route to be dealt with was Stormont. By 26 March 1942 sufficient new trolleybuses had been deliv-

ered to allow both legs of the route, the one via Queen's Bridge and the other via Albert Bridge, to be converted. At the request of the Northern Ireland Government the route was extended from the old tram terminus at Massey Avenue to serve the new Parliament Buildings. The Government paid for the capital cost of the additional overhead equipment and modified the roads in the Stormont estate to make them suitable for trolleybus operation. An intermediate terminus was built at Belmont Drive, which was capable of holding at least six trolleybuses, and a further turning circle was erected at the former tram terminus at the Massey Avenue entrance to Stormont. Vehicles destined for Parliament Buildings showed 'PARLIAMENT BUILDINGS' on their destination blinds, while those turning at Massey Avenue showed simply 'STORMONT'.

In general trolleybuses served Parliament Buildings during normal working hours, while buses working at weekends and evenings generally turned at Massey Avenue. Although both termini were served by both 'legs' of the route, there was a tendency for a number of years for the majority of Parliament Buildings vehicles to go via Queen's Bridge, while most of those via Albert Bridge turned at Massey Avenue. At the City Centre end trolleybuses followed the same route as the Cregagh and Castlereagh services.

The introduction of trolleybuses to the Dundonald route followed on 16 November 1942. Sufficient vehicles were available only for the Queen's Bridge 'leg', and the Albert Bridge service had to wait until 8 March 1943. The Dundonald terminus consisted of an anticlockwise turning loop in the mouth of the Comber and Upper Newtownards Roads just outside John Bell's pub, later known as the Elk Inn, and this remained unchanged until the end of trolleybus operation on the route in 1963. A turning circle was also constructed in the mouth of the Upper Newtownards Road and Knock Road junction, but this was later altered to an 'off-road' turning circle at Ormiston Park.

A further facility for short workings was introduced at Holywood Arches. Trolleybuses could turn at this point by turning left from Upper Newtownards Road into Grampian Avenue, and left again into Holywood Road. Vehicles on the former service showed 'KNOCK ROAD' on their destination blinds, while those serving the latter point showed 'CONNSWATER', later 'HOLYWOOD ARCHES'.

Glentoran Football Club had its ground at 'The Oval'. While trolleybuses could not reach the ground itself, a long passing siding was erected from Albertbridge Road around the Ropeworks curve and down the Newtownards Road. Although early trolleybus destination blinds did have 'OVAL GROUNDS' as a display, trolleybuses on this special service generally showed 'CONNSWATER'.

The final vehicle from the batch of 88 was delivered on 6 October 1943, and apart from the two utility Sunbeams delivered shortly afterwards, Belfast was to receive no more trolleybuses until after the war; this effectively stopped any further route conversions. However, traffic congestion had been steadily building up in the city centre during the previous few years, and a particular problem had arisen in Donegall Place. Although private motoring had been very severely curtailed as a result of petrol rationing, the increase in commercial and public transport was causing concern. For instance, the number of trolleybuses traversing the High Street/Donegall Place/Chichester Street loop had reached 75 vehicles per hour during the day, rising to 97 per hour during the morning and evening peaks.

Samuel Carlisle came up with the recommendation to re-route Albert Bridge trolleybuses inwards via Victoria Street and Chichester Street to a stand in Donegall Square East, then outward via May Street and Victoria Street to rejoin the usual route; he suggested that Queen's Bridge trolleybuses continue as before. After some acrimonious discussion and several counter-suggestions from the Committee, this was accepted and agreement was given to seeking the necessary legislation. However, the Ministry of Home Affairs balked at the proposal to wire Donegall Square East and May Street on the grounds that the left-hand turns from Chichester Street into Donegall Square East and that from Donegall Square East into May Street were too tight. The Ministry also pointed out that the original problem lay in traffic congestion in Donegall Place, and this had been alleviated to a great extent by the relocation of some bus stops. The Corporation was also reminded that the post-war planning commission was likely to recommend a central ring road for Belfast, within which public transport would not be allowed to operate. Donegall Square East and May Street would be within this ring and would therefore become 'non-public-transport' streets. Finally the Ministry pointed out that the air raid shelters already in these streets would cause problems to trolleybus operation.

Carlisle argued forcefully against the objections, asserting that the turns into and out of Donegall Square East were no more difficult than many others in the city; that the streets were no narrower than several on which trolleybuses were operating at present; and that the air raid shelters and static water tank would not interfere with the trolleybuses. Within a few weeks the Ministry backed down and the necessary overhead was erected at a cost of £7,300.

The new arrangements came into use on 5 June 1944 - Belfast trolleybuses invaded Donegall Square East just one day before the Allies invaded Normandy! The Methodist Church and Harry Ferguson Ltd had premises in Donegall Square East and both protested vehemently, the former because the trolleybuses interfered with their customers on Sundays, and the latter because they did so for the rest of the week. To buy time Carlisle agreed to review the arrangements in six months, but by then everybody had become used to the situation, which remained in force until 1958. At that time a major reorganisation of the city centre traffic changed the nature of the problem.

For the next two years there was very little change in the pattern of trolleybus operation other than a continued increase in the number of passengers carried. Although the greater parts of the Bloomfield and Ormeau routes had been wired for trolleybuses at the same time as the other East Belfast routes, no further expansion of the service occurred then. However, urgent major sewer works required attention in Botanic Avenue and the tram service

was suspended to facilitate them, and temporary bus service to Ormeau via Botanic Avenue substituted. After the engineering works were completed the trams did not return, and the temporary bus service became permanent. Except for the Ravenhill Road route in 1940, this was the first major tram route to be replaced by motor buses. The Cromac Street portion of the Ormeau route remained tram-operated.

Post-war expansion

As the war ended and the country returned to peace, the Transport Department took stock. Demobilisation was under way, and although petrol rationing was still in force, the prospect of an easing of restrictions encouraged people to think of travelling for pleasure again. For many years the slogan 'Is your journey really necessary?' (and the severe overcrowding) discouraged any leisure travel.

The Department considered how it had been affected by the war. In terms of direct damage to plant and equipment, it had come off fairly lightly. No trolleybuses had been lost, although Antrim Road tram depot had received a direct hit and several trams had been destroyed. Track and overhead had been damaged in air raids but had been quickly repaired.

During the year ended 31 March 1946 almost 254 million passengers were carried, of which 25 per cent were carried by trolleybus, 17 per cent by motor bus and the remaining 58 per cent by tram. The fleet strengths were 104 trolleybuses, 146 buses and 325 trams. However, vehicles, track and overhead had received only the bare minimum of maintenance during the war, and the trams and tram track in particular were in a poor state.

In February 1946 the Transport Committee reviewed its policy of route conversion. The greatly increased tram service coupled with sustained gross overcrowding and poor maintenance indicated that it would be sensible to convert the North Belfast routes as a matter of urgency. Shortly after his demobilisation, Colonel McCreary, as he had become, recommended the introduction of trolleybuses to the Glengormley, Greencastle, Cliftonville and Oldpark routes as soon as possible at an estimated cost of £661,000.

In 1946 12 semi-utility Sunbeams entered service, and this allowed consideration to be given to finishing the conversions in East Belfast. On 6 May trolleybuses appeared on the Bloomfield route for the first time; it had originally been intended to extend this route from the tram terminus at the Bloomfield Road/North Road junction along North Road itself to the junction with Upper Newtownards Road. There would have been a reverser at Cyprus Avenue and a single pair of wires allowing trolleybuses to turn left into Upper Newtownards Road and return to the city centre. However, it was felt that the bridge on North Road over the Belfast & County Down Railway would not be strong enough to support trolleybuses, and in the event a turning circle was constructed in the junction of Bloomfield Road and North Road. Trolleybuses followed the tram route almost exactly. From the city centre departure point at Donegall Square East they went via May Street, Victoria Street, East Bridge Street, Albert Bridge, Woodstock Road, Beersbridge Road and Bloomfield Road, crossing the Castlereagh route at Castlereagh Street. Trams used the live trolleybus overhead for most of the route, but at the terminus a separate tram wire branched from the trolleybus wire to allow the trams access to their crossover.

During the next two years a number of Guy BTXs were delivered, the first 24 bearing the pre-war FZ registration mark originally reserved for those AECs cancelled in 1940. On 19 April 1948 the tram service to Ormeau Road via Cromac Street was replaced by trolleybuses operating on a 5-minute frequency. As with Bloomfield, most of the route had had trolleybus overhead wiring installed for several years, and the trams used the 'positive' or 'live' trolleybus wire.

The original plan had been to turn trolleybuses at the suburban end by routing them outward from the tram terminus at Hampton Park via Saintfield Road, Newtownbreda Road (now known as Belvoir Road) and inward via Church Road, but Down County Council objected on the grounds that Church Road was unsuitable for heavy vehicles. Since a suitable location could not be found adjacent to the tram terminus, a turning circle was built on Saintfield Road on a site currently occupied by the Supermac shopping centre. This terminus was referred to in Belfast Corporation timetables and publicity material as 'Fortbreda', although destination screens invariably showed 'ORMEAU'. An intermediate turning circle was built at Rosetta at the junction of Ormeau and Ravenhill Roads.

In the immediate post-war period Belfast Corporation was going through one of its anti-public-transport phases, and pressure was exerted to ban all public transport vehicles from the city centre on the grounds that they caused traffic congestion. One suggestion was that bus and trolleybus routes should be terminated on the edge of the central area. Partly because of this pressure, McCreary agreed to use Victoria Square as the city centre terminus for Ormeau Road trolleybuses. Victoria Square had been wired before 1948 as part of the East Belfast scheme, and trolleybuses could be turned there from either direction. Approaching from Ormeau there was an electric frog that was operated to turn left into Victoria Square. From the Queen's Bridge direction a hand-operated frog allowed trolleybuses to turn right into the Square (it was normally set for 'straight through'). The exit from the Square was also a hand-operated frog normally set for the Ormeau Road trolleys to turn right.

Glengormley was the next tram route to be converted to trolleybuses, and was perhaps one of the most difficult for a number of reasons. The city end of the route had its services split between Carlisle Circus and Duncairn Gardens, and large portions of each 'leg' of the route required to be served by both trams and trolleybuses for some years. Specifically Crumlin Road and Oldpark trams would continue to use Royal Avenue, Donegall Street and Clifton Street, while Greencastle cars would continue to operate on York Street.

Tramcars had traditionally used crossovers on short workings at a number of points along the route where trolleybus turning circles could not easily be constructed, for example Waterworks, Chichester Park and Bellevue. There was no depot on the route that would be suitable

for conversion to accommodate trolleybuses. The one at Salisbury Avenue was very difficult for tram access, and trolleybuses could not have made the turns; besides which, the depot was just too small. In addition there were unusual peak traffic patterns to Bellevue, the Zoo and the Floral Hall, and the main Antrim Road itself was liable to subsidence. Finally the overhead wiring required at the Donegall Street/Royal Avenue junction would need to be very complex to accommodate both trams and trolleybuses.

However, Robert McCreary was in no way put off by these difficulties and determined to go ahead with the conversion. The man who had succeeded in building railways under fire from the Wehrmacht was not going to be thwarted by a few technical difficulties! Objections from Belfast Rural District Council and the Ministry of Home Affairs precluded building a turning circle at Glengormley, so he arranged to purchase some land between Church Road and Antrim Road to the South of Carnmoney Road on which he built a reverser. The entrance to the reverser was narrow, but with care two trolleybuses could just pass. Since the land was privately owned, BCT was able to put up a notice banning other vehicles from using it.

The terminal facilities at the city end of the route were also complex. Trolleybuses operated outward from the stop in Castle Place via High Street and Bridge Street to Lower Donegall Street. Trolleybuses going via Carlisle Circus then entered Upper Donegall Street, Clifton Street and Antrim Road, while those routed via Duncairn Gardens went via York Street and Brougham Street.

It was felt essential to provide an intermediate turning point as near as possible to the former Chichester Park tram terminus. McCreary's first plan was to construct a one-way loop in Strathmore Park, Coolmoyne Park and North Circular Road, which trolleybuses would use in an anticlockwise direction. Local residents, however, successfully lobbied members of the Corporation and the scheme was dropped. The second plan was to erect a turning circle adjacent to the Strathmore Park gate lodge at the entrance to Belfast Castle on land owned by the Corporation. This was agreed to, but could not be completed in time for the conversion, which was planned for 24 January 1949. As a temporary expedient a reverser was installed in Strathmore Park, used only until the new turning circle was completed on 22 February 1950.

The pattern of operation was that vehicles operated alternately via Carlisle Circus and Glengormley, every second vehicle on each 'leg' going to Glengormley and the remainder turning at Antrim Road, as the new turning circle became known. Effectively this gave a 5-minute service throughout the route with a 2½-minute service between Duncairn Gardens and Strathmore Park.

In addition to the reverser at Strathmore Park, McCreary constructed an unusually complex turning circle at Carlisle Circus, at which vehicles could be turned from either direction, and a reverser at Churchill Street, which was mainly used during the 'Twelfth of July' celebrations.

On summer Sundays and other holidays large numbers of people would spend the day at Bellevue Zoo. The pattern of traffic would be from the city centre to the Zoo in the morning and in the other direction in the late afternoon. There was also a dance in the Floral Hall on Saturday evenings, which attracted huge numbers of young people. Initially no turning facilities were provided at Bellevue and the additional trolleybuses for these special services were required to reverse at Glengormley, causing chaos to the regular buses.

Eventually a small turning circle was built on the seaward side of the Antrim Road near the Zoo entrance, and a regular service established from Castle Junction. However, as the holiday crowds increased in the post-war years this soon became inadequate. As it finally evolved, the layout of the overhead wiring was quite complex. A long siding to the north of the turning circle trailed into the turning circle itself, while a similar siding was built to the south. This meant that a number of services could be worked independently; these included the 'normal' Castle Junction to Glengormley service and an additional Castle Junction to Bellevue service. There was also the 'tea-time' service: in order to park enough trolleybuses at Bellevue to cope with the massive exodus at tea-time, a number of vehicles would be run up to Bellevue, turned in the circle and 'stacked' in the southern loop. This permitted both the normal Glengormley and Bellevue services to operate without interference from the Bellevue specials. At very busy times a further batch of trolleys could be 'stacked' in the northern siding. They could enter the loop and park behind the southern 'stack' as the latter boarded passengers and left for the city centre. Finally there was a special Carlisle Circus to Bellevue service; on particularly busy days trolleybuses filled up at Castle Junction and were unable to pick up the regular passengers along the Antrim Road, so the additional Carlisle Circus to Bellevue was operated to alleviate this problem.

The final problem was the complex wiring at Donegall Street/Royal Avenue. This was solved by re-routing inward trolleybuses via Clifton Street, North Queen Street, Frederick Street and York Street, thereby removing the need for wiring to accommodate the right-hand turn from Lower Donegall Street into Royal Avenue. If Parliament Buildings was the most photogenic trolleybus route in Belfast, Glengormley was arguably the most interesting!

The next route for conversion was Greencastle. The trams had operated only to the City Boundary at Mount Street, and the intention was to find a trolleybus turning circle as near there as possible. Although in law the Corporation was allowed to operate up to a quarter of a mile beyond the City Boundary, McCreary was unable to find a suitable site for a trolleybus turning circle within the statutory area. He did identify a piece of land about 250 metres beyond the limit allowed by the Act, which he could rent for £50 per annum, and the Committee agreed to his proposal to do so.

However, problems were not slow in coming in the shape of the Ulster Transport Authority (UTA), which operated the green country buses. The UTA jealously guarded its territory and refused to allow Belfast Corporation to pick up or set down passengers outside the Belfast Transport Area (BTA). The general arrangement was that the UTA could not set down passengers on the outward journey within the BTA, nor could they allow passengers to board incoming UTA buses once the BTA boundary was crossed. Equally the BCT had no authority

to carry passengers in either direction outside the BTA. The UTA and the BCT met to resolve the problem, but neither was prepared to give way. Not only was the 250 metres between the BTA and the turning circle very lucrative in the early 1950s because of the Merville Garden Village housing scheme located near the turning circle, but also both organisations were aware that any precedent created at Greencastle could have serious effects elsewhere. The matter was complicated by the fact that the BCT fare structure favoured those passengers affected, and the service was more frequent. The BCT therefore enjoyed considerable public support.

A variety of solutions was suggested, including protective fares, shared receipts, dually valid tickets and reciprocal running powers. None of these was acceptable to both parties, and McCreary took the bold step of introducing the trolleybuses to Whitehouse on 2 October 1950 in the absence of any agreement. Although the trolleybuses operated to the turning circle at Whitehouse they carried no passengers between there and the BTA boundary at Whitehouse Post Office. Until the trolleybuses arrived the dispute did not directly affect the public, but being prevented in wet weather from boarding vehicles standing at the terminus understandably caused much bad feeling. In the event agreement was not reached until 18 February 1952, and even then the BCT was required to charge an additional penny for the 250 metres that was equally divided between the BCT and the UTA! This unsatisfactory situation gave rise to this stretch of road becoming known as 'The Merville Gap'.

Additional turning points were established at Fortwilliam at an 'off-road' turning circle beside the tram depot, and at Grove Park in the mouth of the North Queen Street/York Road junction. Although trolleybuses could not cope with the tram bay at the LMS station, a passing siding was installed just north of the station and another near Seaview Park, the home of the Crusaders football team. The Greencastle route was linked with Falls Road, becoming the first cross-town trolleybus service in Belfast. The all-day service to Falls Road was every 3 minutes, while Greencastle enjoyed a 3-minutes service at peak periods, with an off-peak service of 6 minutes to the terminus and an additional 6-minute service to Fortwilliam.

Colonel McCreary announced his retirement in May 1951, giving his reasons as personal and financial. He was succeeded by the Rolling Stock Engineer, Joseph Mackle, whose professional life had been spent among buses, and he formally assumed his duties in September. An interesting candidate was Mackle's assistant, Robin Adams; at only 40 years of age he was considered rather young and was not short-listed.

In 1947 the Cliftonville tram service had been replaced by buses. On 30 April 1951 it was converted to trolleybuses and extended from the tram terminus at Cliftonville Circus along the Oldpark Road and Ballysillan Road to a new turning circle at the corner of Joanmount Gardens and Ballysillan Road. An intermediate turning circle was completed at Cliftonville Circus. Trolleybuses going to Joanmount showed 'CARR'S GLEN VIA CLIFTONVILLE ROAD', while those turning at Cliftonville Circus displayed 'CLIFTONVILLE'.

Carr's Glen was linked with Cregagh to become the second (and last) cross-town trolleybus service. There was a 2-minute peak service to Cregagh, reducing to 4 minutes during the remainder of the day. This was twice the frequency to Carr's Glen, so every second Cregagh trolleybus operated only to the City Hall.

After the war private motoring continued to increase and the decision was taken to introduce the first major one-way street scheme in central Belfast. This was at Donegall Quay and involved all traffic (including trolleybuses) travelling via Victoria Street, Queen's Square, Donegall Quay and Ann Street in a clockwise direction. The scheme came into operation on 21 September 1952. Tramcars were exempt from the one-way system and continued to turn right from High Street into Victoria Street en route to the Queen's Bridge, protected by a special phase in the traffic lights.

The scheme was so successful that a similar arrangement was introduced in the Cromac Square area on 19 April 1953. Traffic (again including trolleybuses) operated clockwise around the East Bridge Street, Cromac Street, May Street and Oxford Street loop, and trams were again exempt for their last few months of operation.

For several years there had been considerable pressure to extend the transport network to the new housing estates that were being built around the city, but the Transport Department was constrained both by the shortage of buses (both trolley and diesel) and by the difficulty in obtaining suitable plots of land for turning circles. A service was provided along the Glen Road from its junction with Falls Road to a turning circle on the out-of-town side at Binigan Drive, opposite St Theresa's Church. The 3-minute service to Falls Road was split, giving a 6-minute frequency on each route.

On Monday 24 November 1952 trolleybuses replaced buses on the Holywood Road. They operated from the stand at Donegall Square East to a turning circle near where the Sydenham Bypass now joins the Holywood Road. Unusually, Holywood Road was built with laybys at several of the bus stops.

In 1952 the trolleybus fleet had been strengthened by the purchase of 11 second-hand vehicles from Wolverhampton, and this allowed several more short route extensions. On 26 April 1953 a spur was opened from the Shore Road to the Throne Hospital on the Whitewell Road, and on 20 June 1954 the Falls Road route was extended by about 300 metres from the reverser at Fruithill Park to a new turning circle at Casement Park.

The mid-1950s were perhaps the high point for Belfast trolleybuses. In the year ended 31 March 1954, 245 vehicles carried about 108 million passengers over almost 8½ million miles. This was as much as the buses and trams combined.

On 18 May 1959 trolleybuses replaced diesel buses on the Whiterock Road. Overhead was erected from the City Cemetery on the Falls Road to the terminus at the junction of Divismore Crescent and Springfield Road via Whiterock Road and Springfield Road. Initially trolleybuses used the turning circle in an anticlockwise direction, but this was altered to clockwise in the early 1960s.

'Britain's Biggest Bus Stop'

Reference has already been made to the increase in traffic congestion and the solutions based on the one-way traffic schemes at Donegall Quay and Cromac Square. Notwithstanding these measures, the traffic congestion got progressively worse. A firm of traffic consultants was retained whose main recommendation was to establish a one-way scheme based on the City Hall. Robin Adams, then Acting Deputy General Manager, felt that the scheme should be more wide-ranging, and successfully argued that it should include Chichester Street, May Street, Howard Street and Wellington Place. Adams realised that a major criterion for success would be the degree to which the trolleybuses were able to adapt to the new traffic patterns, by contributing to the smooth flow of vehicles in the city centre.

Clough Smith was invited to tender for the massive overhead wiring alterations needed for the trolleybuses. It was intended to carry out as much preparatory work as possible and concentrate the first phase of the changeover during the weekend of 5/6 July 1958, with the final phase and traffic re-routing on the following weekend. The traditional Orange Parades of that weekend were not conducive to massive construction work to the trolleybus overhead, and the final phase was therefore postponed until Sunday 20 July.

In essence the resulting overhead line work gave the trolleybuses every bit as much flexibility as the motor buses, not only as regards passenger safety when boarding and alighting, but also in having sufficient sidings to allow most routes to have their own 'loading bays', thereby causing minimal traffic disruption. Adams appreciated the importance of preparing the trolleybus crews for the changeover and he produced a comprehensive instruction booklet detailing the way to deal with all possible traffic movements for trolleybuses in the city centre. Most of the new bus stops were located around the City Hall, which acquired a forest of traction poles and the nickname 'Britain's Biggest Bus Stop'. The Holywood Road service was converted to motor buses on 1 June 1958 and the overhead wiring exclusive to that route was not included in the new scheme. On 26 October 1958 the Ormeau Road route was abandoned to motor buses and the wiring modified again.

The flexibility allowed by Adams's scheme was remarkable. If Belfast had the largest trolleybus fleet in the British Isles outside London, the City Hall overhead wiring was certainly the most complex in the country, if not the world. Donegall Square North with six pairs of parallel wires was quite amazing!

The Twelfth of July

The 'Twelfth of July' in Northern Ireland is not only a national holiday, but an occasion when many parades are held throughout the province. The largest of these is in Belfast, when upwards of 20,000 Orangemen march from Carlisle Circus to 'The Field', originally at Finaghy but latterly moved to Edenderry. The route through Belfast is via Clifton Street, Donegall Street, Royal Avenue, Donegall Place, Donegall Square North and West,

Bedford Street, Shaftesbury Square and Lisburn Road. From Carlisle Circus to Donegall Square West the parade passed along trolleybus routes. As the parade took several hours to pass a given point and was joined at several places by smaller processions from other parts of the city, a detailed operational plan was devised to minimise the disruption to trolleybus services.

The only two cross-town services, Cregagh to Carr's Glen and Falls Road or Glen Road to Greencastle or Whitewell, were severed and terminated just outside the city centre. Trolleybus routes via Queen's Bridge originally turned at Victoria Square, as did those via Albert Bridge. Later, when the one-way loops at Donegall Quay and Cromac Square were constructed, the buses used these instead.

West Belfast services on the trunk Falls Road used a reverser at the Queen Street/Castle Street junction, while York Street trolleybuses (Greencastle, Whitewell and Duncairn Gardens) used one at the Frederick Street/York Street junction. Trolleybuses on Lower Antrim Road routes (Antrim Road, Bellevue, Glengormley and Carr's Glen) used the reverser at the junction of Churchill Street and Antrim Road until the procession had cleared Carlisle Circus. Once the Circus was free again the service was extended to there. These diversions lasted perhaps three hours in the morning and slightly less in the afternoon. Inspectors were on hand at most of the temporary termini both to help with possible problems and to advise the travelling public of the arrangements.

Closure

From the point of view of a chief executive of a public transport undertaking, the 1950s appeared to be a period of hope, expansion and prosperity. The arguments appeared to be about which authority had the right to provide services and about which mode of public transport was the best or cheapest or most effective. By the end of the decade, however, it had begun to be appreciated that the real debate was about public transport versus private transport. In Belfast the numbers of passengers peaked in 1948 at over 263 million. By 1957 the number had dropped to just over 200 million.

The late 1950s saw serious consideration being given to the future of trolleybuses in Belfast. The original stock was then approaching 20 years of age, and they were criticised for being inflexible, increasingly expensive to run, and limited to operating routes equipped with overhead that was costly to maintain. London Transport's decision in 1954 to abandon its vast trolleybus network (45 per cent of all trolleybuses in the UK were in London) ensured that manufacturing development would virtually cease, spare parts would become increasingly difficult to obtain, and the other systems would have little choice but to follow suit.

On 1 June 1958 the Holywood Road trolleybus route was 'temporarily' replaced by motor buses to allow the construction of the Sydenham Bypass, but in fact the 'suspension' soon became permanent. At less than six years old, it was to be Belfast's shortest-lived trolleybus route. On 26 October of the same year the Ormeau Road route

was abandoned to make way for the redevelopment of the area around the terminus.

In 1958 the Transport Committee agreed to buy four experimental vehicles to help decide the future direction of public transport. Three were motor buses - an AEC Bridgemaster, a Leyland Atlantean and a Dennis Loline - and the fourth a new trolleybus, No 246 (2206 OI), a four-wheel Sunbeam with BTH electrical equipment and Harkness 68-seater bodywork. It was hoped that 246 would be the forerunner of a fleet of 100 new trolleybuses, but regretfully this fine vehicle was to be Belfast's last trolleybus. In 1959 the decision was formally taken to abandon the trolleybus system.

The ex-Wolverhampton vehicles had all been withdrawn by 1956, the original 14 by 1958, and the final utility Sunbeams were scrapped in 1960. Since the closure of services to Holywood Road and Ormeau Road there was an adequate number of trolleybuses for the remainder of the routes.

Although the dispute between the UTA and the BCT over the Greencastle route had been resolved, the Corporation disliked the additional administrative requirements associated with sharing the revenue and determined to withdraw from the UTA's territory as soon as possible. Not surprisingly, therefore, the Greencastle trolleybus route was the next to be converted to motor buses, which were diverted up Mill Road to a new turning circle inside the Belfast Transport Area.

Traffic congestion continued to cause concern and trolleybuses were increasingly blamed for playing a major contributory part. Traffic consultants were again brought in, and they recommended that a new bridge be built over the River Lagan adjacent to the existing Queen's Bridge. The recommendation was accepted and the question of whether trolleybuses should be included in the new scheme was considered. Robin Adams battled hard for their inclusion, but was successful only to the point of getting sockets for traction poles installed in the approaches to the bridge.

An interesting side-light on Belfast politics was the controversy over the name of the new bridge. A conductor was reprimanded apparently for whistling 'The Sash' - a party tune that could give offence to certain people. In his defence he argued that in fact he was whistling a popular song of the period, which just happened to be to the tune of 'The Sash':

'Oh they've built a bridge in Belfast - it's causing quite a stir;
The name that they have chosen - I'll never know for sure
Which name has been selected - I never had a vote
And now the politicians have each other by the throat.

Is it Carson or Elizabeth, O'Neill or Sean Lemass?
I've heard it called by many a name, but I'm going to let that pass.
Is it Paisley, Wolfe Tone, Lagan Bridge? Somebody called it Paul.
I think we'd be better off if we had no bridge at all!'

Since the song had recently been issued as a record, the conductor's explanation was accepted - but only just! (Incidentally, Carson was an Ulster Unionist leader in the 1920s; Elizabeth refers to the Queen of England; O'Neill was a former Prime Minister of Northern Ireland; Lemass was a former Prime Minister of the Irish Republic; and Paisley is still around! Wolfe Tone, although Protestant, was an Irish Nationalist leader of the late 18th century, and Paul was the Pope in the 1960s. The Lagan is the river that flows under the bridge. The name finally chosen was 'Queen Elizabeth II Bridge'.)

The decision was taken to withdraw all services from East Belfast and this was accomplished during 1963. Castlereagh was the first to go on 20 January, quickly followed by Stormont and Dundonald on 30 March. Cregagh, Bloomfield and Carr's Glen were all converted to bus operation on 14 October. Thus within nine months East Belfast, the home of Belfast trolleybuses, was reduced to depot workings only. Both Short Strand and Haymarket retained traction wires, although the former was closed for trolleybus operational purposes in March. The majority of the AEC trolleybuses were withdrawn from service in 1963, but No 98 was preserved by the Corporation, prepared to 'ex-works' condition and presented to The Ulster Folk and Transport Museum later that year.

Glengormley was closed in two stages. On 13 June 1965 the all-day services were replaced by buses; by agreement with the UTA these were extended as far as Carnmoney, Ballyhenry and Roughfort, which is still very much out in the country. From June 1965 trolleybuses provided a peak-hour service to Glengormley, but from February 1966 all services on the Antrim Road were provided by motor buses.

In effect this left only two routes, Whitewell via Shore Road and the trunk Falls Road, with the two branches to Whiterock and Glen Road. Although greatly simplified from the early days, a surprisingly large amount of wiring remained in the city centre and eastwards, which was used only for depot workings.

The closing ceremony

The final day of trolleybus operation in Belfast was Sunday 12 May 1968. Because of reasons to do with Sunday observance, the Corporation Transport Department organised the official last day celebrations on Saturday 11 May. Guys 112 and 168 were used with Sunbeam 246 on the trip from the City Hall to Falls Park turning circle and back, and the day was concluded with a civic reception.

The National Trolleybus Association (NTA) organised a farewell tour on Sunday - the actual last day of operation - which succeeded in covering almost every piece of overhead wiring in the city. At about 1.00 pm Guy 112 left Haymarket Depot for Short Strand Depot and journeyed to Short Strand, Falls Road, Glen Road, Whitewell and Whiterock, returning to Haymarket Depot in time for tea. During the trip several photographic stops were made.

The 'final' final tour organised by the NTA left Haymarket at about 11.00 pm and operated to Falls Road, Castle Junction, Whitewell and City Hall, returning to Haymarket at about 1.00 am. As the depot gates closed behind 168, Belfast was without electric public transport for the first time in 63 years. It was truly the end of an era.

═══ FLEET SUMMARY ═══

BELFAST'S trolleybus fleet eventually grew to 246 vehicles, although there was a maximum of 245 in service at any one time. With the exception of the vehicles bought from Wolverhampton, all vehicles were new and none was sold for service elsewhere. The fleet numbering system was simplicity itself: the trolleybuses were numbered from 1 to 246. Vehicles bore the same fleet number throughout their lives.

1-14 (EZ 7889-EZ 7902)
As the first trolleybus route was constructed on an experimental basis, the initial batch of vehicles was a very 'mixed bag'. The idea was to determine the most suitable combination of chassis, body and electrical equipment for Belfast conditions.

They were delivered early in 1938 and used initially for driver training; they then operated the Falls Road service from March 1938. There were seats for 68 passengers, 36 upstairs and 32 in the lower saloon. All vehicles were six-wheelers.

Fleet No	Chassis	Electrical equipment	Body
1, 2	AEC	English Electric	Harkness
3	Crossley	Metro-Vick	Crossley
4	Crossley	Metro-Vick	Harkness
5, 6	Daimler	Metro-Vick	Harkness
7	Guy BTX	English Electric	Park Royal
8	Guy BTX	English Construction	Harkness
9, 10	Karrier E6A	Crompton-West	Harkness
11, 12	Leyland TTB	GEC	Leyland
13, 14	Sunbeam MS2	British Thompson-Houston	Cowieson

15-102 (FZ 7800-FZ 7887)
In 1939 114 trolleybuses were ordered for the East Belfast services, but the outbreak of war in September required the diversion of Britain's manufacturing capacity to armaments, and Belfast's order was summarily reduced to 88 by the Ministry of War Transport. The six-wheel chassis

were built by the Associated Equipment Company (AEC), and the electrical equipment was by the General Electric Company (GEC). The Belfast firm of Harkness built the bodies on Park Royal frames and the completed vehicles were delivered between 1940 and 1943. The seating layout was identical to the original batch.

The fleet numbers 103 to 128 and registration numbers FZ 7886 to FZ 7913 had been reserved for the 26 vehicles 'short'. The numbers were subsequently allocated to the Guys (see below).

129 and 130 (GZ 1620 and GZ 1621)
These two vehicles were the only trolleybuses delivered to Belfast with the full rigours of utility bodywork, and they were spartan indeed! Delivered in 1943, they were Sunbeam Ws with British Thompson-Houston electrical equipment and, unusually for Belfast, Park Royal bodywork. The austerity specification to which they were built included a shorter four-wheel chassis and only 56 seats, of which 30 were upstairs and 26 downstairs.

103-128 and 143-186 (FZ 7888-FZ 7913 and GZ 8507-GZ 8550)
For the North Belfast extensions of Carr's Glen and Whitehouse more trolleybuses were required. The Corporation therefore bought 70 Guy BTXs with GEC electrical equipment and Harkness bodywork. Like the AECs they were six-wheelers and had a similar seating arrangement. The Guys were delivered during 1948 and 1949, with the final two (185 and 186) coming in 1950. It is noteworthy that these were the only Guy BTXs built after the end of the war.

131-142 (GZ 2802-GZ 2813)
These 12 semi-utility Sunbeam Ws had BTH electrical equipment and Harkness bodywork. Although there was some easing of strict utility regulations after the war, allowing a slightly less 'angular' appearance, this batch of trolleybuses was built on four-wheel chassis and seating remained restricted to 56. The vehicles entered service in 1946.

187-210 (GZ 8551-GZ 8574)
The next batch of buses to enter service was built by the British United Traction Co (BUT). This company had been formed in 1946 as a merger between the trolleybus interests of AEC and Leyland. There were 24 vehicles in this group, all of which went into service during 1950. There was little apparent difference from previous deliveries; electrical equipment was supplied by GEC and the bodies were the by now standard Harkness 68-seaters.

235-245 (DDA 182 and DDA 986-DDA 995)
In the early 1950s there was a push to replace the remaining tram routes by trolleybuses. However, new trolleybuses could not be built as quickly as the Corporation required and the decision was taken to buy 11 vehicles from Wolverhampton Corporation Transport, numbered in their fleet as 282 and 286 to 295. They were Sunbeam MF2s with electrical equipment by Metro-Vick. Six vehicles (numbered 235-240 in the Belfast fleet) had Park Royal bodywork with 28 seats upstairs and 26 downstairs, while the remaining five (241-245) had Roe bodies. Although all the vehicles had 54 seats, the Roe-bodied buses had one more seat upstairs and one fewer downstairs! 235 was new to Wolverhampton in 1940 and the remainder in 1942. The power and brake pedals were altered to conform to the 'Belfast standard', and modifications were made to the destination layouts. They were withdrawn between 1954 and 1956.

211-234 (OZ 7313-OZ 7336)
The final batch of trolleybuses to be built for Belfast Corporation was 24 BUT 9641Ts, again with GEC electrical equipment and a more modern-looking Harkness 68-seater body. The chassis were new in 1952, but priority was given to building bus bodies for tram replacement and the trolleybuses did not see service until late 1953 (fleet number 211) and 1954 (the rest). These trolleybuses were fitted with twin-track route number blinds and as such were readily distinguished from the earlier vehicles, all of which had single-track blinds.

246 (2206 OI)
This was a Sunbeam F4A with BTH electrical equipment and Harkness 68-seater bodywork, entering service in 1958. It was the only 30-foot-long four-wheel vehicle in the fleet. It was fitted with Lockheed brakes, which were non-standard, and proved difficult to maintain. It was hoped that 246 would be the first of a new batch of trolleybuses for Belfast and there was talk of buying up to 100 vehicles. However, this was not to be and the decision was taken formally in 1959 to convert all the trolleybus routes to diesel bus operation.

THE CITY CENTRE

THIS COMPRISES the area bounded by Queen Street, Royal Avenue, Lower Donegall Street, High Street, Queen's Square, Donegall Quay, Oxford Street, Cromac Square, May Street and Donegall Square West.

Initially the trolleybus overhead wiring was limited to a simple anticlockwise loop around Queen Street, Wellington Place, Donegall Place and Castle Street to provide a turning point for trolleybuses coming from the Falls Road. The addition of the East Belfast routes during the war required a further anticlockwise loop via High Street, Castle Place, Donegall Place, Chichester Street and Victoria Street, together with connections at Castle Junction and Donegall Square North to facilitate trolleybuses moving between Haymarket and Falls Depots.

A second turning facility for the East Belfast routes was introduced in 1944, which used Chichester Street, Donegall Square East and May Street, also in an anticlockwise direction. The introduction of the Glengormley route in 1949 saw overhead wires installed in Royal Avenue and Bridge Street.

However, the City Hall one-way scheme in 1958, and the associated 'sidings' at bus stops, gave the trolleybuses every bit as much flexibility as motor buses. The amount of overhead wiring (and associated traction poles) required to achieve this objective was considerable. The three sets of wires sweeping round Robinson & Cleavers' corner and the six sets of parallel wires in Donegall Square North were most impressive!

The replacement of the Greencastle trolleybuses in 1962 had no effect on the array of wiring in the city centre, but the closure in 1963 of the Castlereagh, Cregagh, Bloomfield, Stormont and Dundonald routes reduced the wiring to that required for depot working only. Falls Road Depot had ceased being operational as far as trolleybuses were concerned in 1947.

Following the major East Belfast closures, Short Strand

Trolleybuses in the city centre, 1948-64.

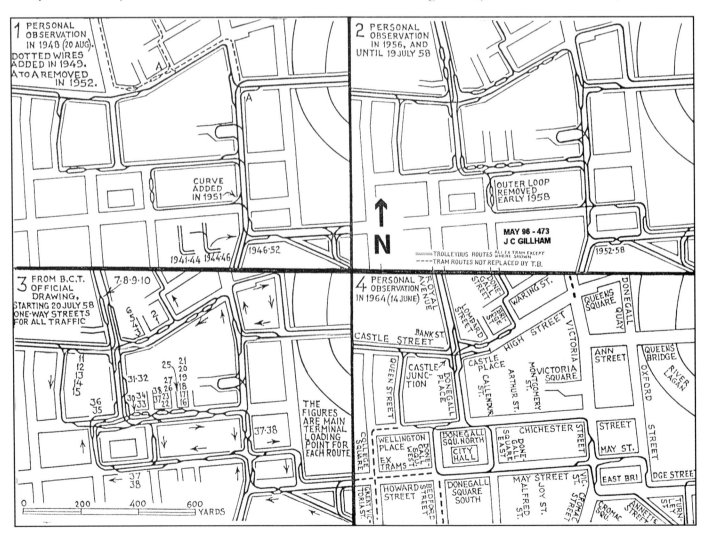

ceased trolleybus operation in 1963, although it retained access wiring from the Albert Bridge and a basic internal layout. From 1963 Haymarket was the only operational trolleybus depot.

Withdrawal of services from Glengormley in 1966 resulted in only minor changes to the traction wiring in the central area.

Since 1938 a set of wires had been provided from Donegall Place into Castle Street, and in 1950 a further set was installed from Royal Avenue. These ran parallel to the others from Castle Junction to Queen Street, at which point they converged. In effect this meant that trolleybuses from Royal Avenue could overtake those from Donegall Place, but not *vice versa*. However, in 1967 a 'figure 8' was installed, which allowed complete flexibility of overtaking. I have not been able to work out why this excellent idea was not carried out 17 years earlier!

When trolleybuses were finally withdrawn on 12 May 1968, the overhead wiring was dismantled with incredible speed in time for the Lord Mayor's Show later that month. Belfast's trolleybus wires in the city centre in their heyday may not have been pretty, but my goodness they were memorable!

Right AEC 105 (FZ 7890) was on Route 1 (Antrim Road via Carlisle Circus) when photographed in Castle Place on 21 April 1965, less than a year before all trolleybuses were withdrawn from the Antrim Road and Glengormley routes.

The motor bus in the left background was one of a hundred Daimlers bought very economically from London Transport in the early 1950s to help speed up tramcar replacement. They were rebodied by the local firm of Harkness Coachbuilders, and the majority gave almost 20 years of additional service, although a number became early victims of terrorist hijackings.

The advertisement on the side of 105 boasts of the three branches of Christie's Wallpapers shops at Rosemary Street, Upper North Street and Shaftesbury Square. The 1994 phone book lists five Belfast branches, with a further ten in various towns around Northern Ireland.

Just to the left of the Daimler bus the Northern Ireland Tourist Board's sign can be seen on the ground floor of the Reform Club building in Royal Avenue. This delightful three-storey red sand-stone building was built between 1883 and 1885 by Maxwell and Tuke of Manchester, as part of the general redevelopment of Royal Avenue, which replaced Hercules Street in the early 1880s. John Collier's at the corner of Castle Place had as its address Royal Avenue and was part of a block built for John Robb in 1881. Robb's intention had been to link with his existing shop in Castle Place. Today the building is a Ravel shoe shop. *Robin Symons*

Right Guy 177 (GZ 8541) entered service in 1948 and was photographed in Castle Place 17 years later, shortly before the Glengormley route was converted to motor buses. Bellevue was a short working of Glengormley and enjoyed a regular Saturday evening timetabled service until 1964. From then until the route was worked completely by motor buses, trolleybuses operated to Bellevue 'as required'.

The two-storey Provincial Bank of Ireland, later Allied Irish and now First Trust Bank, can be seen in background shadow in Royal Avenue, while the Belfast Bank in Castle Place, just to the right of the trolleybus, sports an impressive curved brass plate on the left-hand door pillar. Only just visible in Royal Avenue is one of the then new Daimler Fleetlines delivered in 1963 to replace the ageing trolleybus fleet. The trolleybus has been prevented from reaching its stop by the Ford Prefect wedged between the bus and the kerb. It was situations like this one that gave trams and trolleybuses the undeserved reputation of causing traffic jams; in fact, it was more often than not the fault of thoughtless private motorists.

The advertisement for McCausland Car Hire on the side of the trolleybus must have been effective - the company is now one of the largest car hire firms in Northern Ireland, although today it is based on the Grosvenor Road. *Robin Symons*

Above Castle Place in the mid-1960s as caught by Robin Symons on a sunny afternoon. Three trolleybuses are on the Antrim Road route and they are all Guy BTXs delivered new in 1948. That nearest the camera is 108 (FZ 7893).

Apart from the registrations and fleet numbers, one way in which the post-war Guys could be distinguished from the wartime AECs was the location of the 'pole'; on the AECs the long bamboo stick, used for retrieving errant trolleypoles, was stored along the nearside of the bus on hooks just below the lower deck windows, while on the Guys it was kept in a tube under the bus. The entrance to the tube is easily visible on 108 below and to the left of the number plate. While this arrangement was clearly neater, a problem arose when the stick needed to be removed from under the bus in a traffic jam. It was about 20 feet (about 7 metres) long and it was necessary to ask the drivers of the vehicles behind to back up in order to get it out! Latterly

additional poles were kept at points on the system where de-wirements were common.

The sign 'BUSES FOR BELLEVUE AND HAZELWOOD' was there to ensure that potential customers were left in no doubt where to get their bus. The Corporation Transport Department owned the Bellevue Zoo at that time.

The large five-storey building next door was Robb's famous department store. John Robb & Co was established at 15 Castle Place in 1861 and gradually expanded to fill the entire site between the Bank and the corner of Lombard Street. The store ceased trading in 1973 and the building was demolished to make way for Donegall Arcade. The building on the right-hand side of the picture belongs to Woolworth and Burton. It was built by Woolworth's 'in-house' Construction Department in 1929-30 and the various stages of erection were recorded by the local photographer Alexander Hogg, much of whose work has been preserved by the Ulster Museum. Apart from superficial changes to the ground floor, the building is easily recognisable today.

The bonnet of an Austin FX3 taxi can just be seen behind the trolleybus, while a Volkswagen 'Beetle' is coming towards Castle Junction. *Robin Symons*

Left In February 1996 the Belfast Bank building on the left has been tastefully restored by the Woolwich Building Society, while the new red-brick building to the right is Donegall Arcade. Burton's half of the Woolworth/Burton building has been renamed the 'Internacionale', but is otherwise little different from the previous photograph. *Mike Maybin*

Above D. A. Jones captured this view of 203 in the mid-1950s. It was a British United Traction (BUT) six-wheeler with GEC electrical equipment and 68-seater Harkness bodywork. In the early days of trolleybuses on the Glengormley route there was no turning circle at Bellevue and destination screens often showed 'BELLEVUE & ZOOLOGICAL GDS' in addition to the terminus at Glengormley. By the time that this photograph was taken the tram overhead wire had been removed, although the rails had not then been lifted.

The old 'NO WAITING' signs are attached to the horizontally painted black and white street lights and the small supplementary rectangular sign adds, unhelpfully to private motorists, 'NO WAITING

AT ANY TIME'. The advertisement for Kellogg's is every bit as relevant today. *D. A. Jones, London Trolleybus Preservation Society*

Below Another view of Castle Place, this time of AEC No 66 on 13 June 1953. The legend 'BELFAST CORPORATION' along the side of the vehicle (black letters with gold shading) began to be omitted from September 1953.

The bunting draped along the window ledge of the Ulster Club is in honour of the Coronation. The Club was designed by Charles Lanyon and, regretfully, demolished in 1981 to be replaced by Calvert House three years later. *John Gillham*

Guy 116 (FZ 7901) in High Street en route to Castlereagh on 6 June 1953 - again the Union flags on the single-storey Northern Bank building are in celebration of the recent Coronation. McCreary tram 411, to the left of the trolleybus, is heading towards Queen's Road to collect homeward-bound shipyard workers. In the background a trolleybus is on route 26, Stormont via Queen's Bridge.

The building to the left with the gable, rather reminiscent of Amsterdam, is Alex Sloan's drapers and house furnishers. It was built in 1935 and managed to escape the bombing that unfortunately destroyed the Albert Hotel to the left and Spackman's merchant tailor and clothier to the right. Spackman's is immortalised in a verse that celebrated the length of time they traded in High Street:

'When I was a lad, I went with my dad, And we both got clad at Spackman's
Now I'm a dad, With many a lad, We all get clad at Spackman's.'

The Albert Clock, directly behind the trolleybus (and leaning slightly to the left) was designed by W. J. Barrie and erected in memory of Prince Albert in 1869 just three years before the first horse tram in Belfast. The two-storey Italianate building sandwiched between the two trolleybuses is the Custom House, built in 1854-57 to the design of Lanyon and Lynn. In the pre-war period the area around the Custom House steps was used as Belfast's equivalent to 'Speakers' Corner' in Hyde Park, London. In its early days the Custom House housed a small rifle range for the use of the Excise men based there!

The traffic sign at the entrance to Queen's Square reads 'TURN LEFT EXCEPT TRAMS'. In 1952 a one-way traffic scheme was introduced in the Donegall Quay area, with traffic being required to use Ann Street, Victoria Street, Queen's Square and Donegall Quay in a clockwise direction. The trams were exempt from this obligation as the cost and disruption involved in relaying the rails would not have been cost-effective, given the trams' life expectancy of less than two years. *John Price*

Right It is not certain when this view of 10 was taken, but given the fact that it shows '9 BALLYHACKAMORE VIA CHICHESTER ST & QUEEN'S BRIDGE' on its destination display, carries no wartime markings and a trade plate is present in the nearside front windscreen, it is probably undergoing trials a few days before the formal opening of the Falls Road route (the 'proper' route 9 at that time).

No 10, a Karrier E6A with Compton-West electrical equipment and 68-seater Harkness bodywork, was one of the original 14 experimental vehicles, although in the event the Corporation standardised on AECs. 'T10' together with 'T9' were destined to become the only two Karriers in the Belfast fleet (in the early days fleet numbers on Belfast trolleybuses were prefixed 'T', although this was dropped on the production AECs delivered from 1940).

The semaphore traffic indicator can easily be seen at the front offside corner, which the driver operated by a switch in the cab; a solenoid pulled it to the horizontal position, not unlike a miniature railway signal. The indicators were made of translucent orange plastic and were illuminated from the inside.

The bus behind T10 is one of the batch bought new in 1934 to replace the 'mixed bag' of 50 buses taken over in 1928 as part of the settlement of the 'Bus War', and is on the Stormont route. The traction poles supporting the trolleybus overhead are the slimmer tramway ones, the one nearest the camera retaining the ornamental scroll to which the span wires were attached.

The building at the corner of Donegall Place on the right was replaced by Donegall House in 1968, while Brands Arcade (built in the early 1930s) is still there, albeit known as Brookmount Buildings. The horse and cart making its leisurely way up Donegall Place helps define this as a 'Thirties' view. *Photographer unknown, courtesy of Billy Montgomery*

Below One of the latest batch of BUTs, 213 is seen in Donegall Place on 15 June 1964. The vehicle is well out from the kerb in preparation for making the very tight left turn into Castle Street. In spite of a 'lead' for the overhead wire, de-wirements were fairly common at this point as evidenced by the protective wire netting at Anderson & McAuley's first floor corner window! The Wolseley parked directly under the blue and white 'NO WAITING AT ANYTIME' sign does not help to ease traffic congestion.

The general outlook of the buildings down Donegall Place has not changed greatly in the intervening 30 years since the photograph was taken. However, the three-storey building to the left with the rounded windows at second floor level was built about 1846 and known as 'Castle Buildings'. It was demolished and replaced by McDonald's and Richards in 1986.

The bus heading down Donegall Place in the direction of the City Hall bears an advertisement for Nambarrie Tea. If anything it is more popular today than in 1964 - it is one of Northern Ireland's top brands.

From left to right the cars in the middle of the road are a Volkswagen 'Beetle', Austin A40, Morris Minor and Ford Consul. Going in the direction of the City Hall is a McWatters battery-powered bread van. At one time most cities in the UK had milk and bread delivered by a battery van; although they were fairly slow moving and required to be charged up at night, they proved very economical to operate on short journeys. *John Gillham*

Left There are very few good-quality photographs of the two wartime utility Sunbeams, 129 and 130. This was taken in Donegall Place probably during the war, as evidenced by the white mudguards and front stripe, which were supposed to help visibility in the dark, although most people thought that they made little difference. Although 129 was equipped with a full display at the front, none at all was provided at the side or rear. The vehicle is heading for Houston Park, a short working of the Castlereagh route. Until 1951, when a major revision took place, most intermediate termini were not allocated separate route numbers, hence 129's expedient display of half way between 1 and 2!

The traffic light to the right has its electricity supplied by means of a wire slung to a convenient traction pole. It was to be several years before traffic signals were supplied by underground cable. *Transport World, courtesy of John Whitehead*

Below This view of Donegall Place was probably taken in the early 1960s, and shows not only three sets of parallel wires, but also three trolleybuses almost abreast! Guy 121 (FZ 7806) is on its way to Castlereagh via Queen's Bridge, correctly displaying route number 31; Guy 156 (GZ 8520) is passing it en route for Stormont; while AEC 47 (FZ 7832) is overtaking it about to make a circuit of the City Hall before returning to Carr's Glen. The majority of Carr's Glen trolleybuses were linked with the Cregagh route, but on Saturday afternoons, particularly when Cliftonville Football Club were playing at home, an additional City Hall to Cliftonville or Carr's Glen service was operated. The destination display reads 'CARR'S GLEN VIA CLIFTONVILLE ROAD' on the top blind, while 'VIA CLIFTONVILLE RD' is helpfully, if rather unnecessarily, repeated on the bottom blind.

The car apparently sandwiched between the trolleybus and the double-deck Guy diesel bus is a Vauxhall. *Robert Mack*

Right A relatively unusual shot of a Rebuild tram (31) and a Guy BTX trolleybus, 114 (FZ 7899), side by side in Royal Avenue at its junction with Castle Place. While it has not been possible to date the picture precisely, it would have been the early 1950s. The tram was unusual as it was one of only a few rebuilds to have retained the full gold lining so late in life; most were lined out in yellow after the war to a much simpler standard.

The trolleybus is on the Glengormley route and about to turn left and take up position on the stand in Castle Place. It is perhaps surprising that the city centre was still gas-lit at that time.

An early form of traffic-light-controlled pedestrian crossing marked out by metal studs in the road is visible in the foreground. *A. Ratcliffe*

Below This view of Guy 126 (FZ 7911) was taken in Royal Avenue towards the end of trolleybus operation in the mid-1960s. The destination screen shows 'FALLS ROAD' while the lower blind displays 'VIA YORK STREET & PASSES NORTHERN COUNTIES RAILWAY'. The trolleybus to the left is also a Guy while the diesel buses are a wartime ex-London Transport Daimler and, further up Royal Avenue, a Daimler Fleetline. It is perhaps slightly ironic that the utility Daimler was bought to hasten the replacement of the trams, while the new Daimler was bought to replace the trolley-buses.

The contrasting advertisements on the far trolleybus for hard and soft refreshments are for Gordon's gin and Schweppes mixers, while that on 126 is for Crown wallpapers and paints, all of whom are still in business. The cars in front of the trolleybus are an Austin FX3 taxi and a Standard, and there is another Standard just outside the Grand Central Hotel. *Robert Mack*

Belfast trolleybuses enjoyed an enviable record for infrequency of de-wirements, but nothing is perfect! In this photograph Sunbeam 222 (OZ 7324) had just 'jumped the points', as railway enthusiasts refer to the overhead frogs. It is heading for Falls Road from Whitewell and was just about to pick up the right-hand pair of wires to position itself for the right turn from Royal Avenue into Castle Street. A very embar-rassed conductor is trying his best to retrieve the trolley boom with his bamboo pole. Behind is Daimler Fleetline 656 (656 FZ), en route to Turf Lodge but trapped by the trolleybus's loss of power. Next to 656 is Guy Arab III 325 (MZ 7423), sitting at the Ormeau stop, having come from Downview Avenue.

The Grand Central Hotel is on the left; its semi-circular canopy was a landmark for many years. The hotel was built about 1892 and was one of the last parts of the 1884 Royal Avenue development. Its 200 luxury bedrooms accommodated several note-

worthy guests over the years, including Winston Churchill, Al Jolson, John McCormick, Paul Robeson and the Lone Ranger; no record exists of where Silver was stabled! It was closed as a hotel in the late 1960s, although it gained a further lease of life as the Army's Headquarters in Belfast until 1980, during which period it was bombed twice. It was used briefly as a retail shopping centre until its demolition in the early 1980s, and the site is currently occupied by Castle Court. The cars outside are an 1100, a Jaguar and an Austin from the Republic of Ireland, while the sign on the first traction pole on the left reads 'SMITHFIELD BUS STATION', which was the UTA's terminal for the country services to the north.

The black, rather forbidding-looking building next door was the General Post Office, which was also incorporated into Castle Court. On the right-hand side Rutherford's chemist shop has become a branch of the Ulster Bank. *Robin Symons*

Top This view was taken in Royal Avenue on 20 April 1965, just over three years before the trolleybuses were completely abandoned. The vehicle at Castle Junction about to turn right into Castle Street en route to Glen Road is 193 (GZ 8557), a BUT 9641T with GEC electrical equipment and 68-seater Harkness bodywork. It was delivered in 1950 and hardly looks its 15 years. The original semaphore trafficators have been replaced by the much more effective flashing lights. The slogan 'Go Modern - Go Gallaher's' is no longer used in company advertising, but Gallaher's Blues, Greens (mild) and Reds (tipped) have been joined by a host of other cigarette brand names in more recent years.

The building immediately behind the Daimler Fleetline bus, the Reform Club of 1885, is still very much there today, although the ground floor is occupied by a building society. The Morris Minor appears to have a minor problem with its left trafficator! *Robin Symons*

Middle This view was taken early in the 1950s, before the end of tramcar operation in Belfast. It shows Guy BTX 149, which carried GEC electrical equipment and 68-seater Harkness bodywork. The location is Royal Avenue, not far from the corner with Donegall Street, and the camera is pointing away from the city centre.

The semaphore trafficator has not returned to its housing, which was rather a problem with them; in an attempt to reduce the incidence of drivers accidentally snapping them off when alighting from the cab, they were later made from a flexible moulded rubber. In fact, the problem was not cured until they were replaced with flashing lights.

The three-storey red-brick building was demolished a number of years ago and has become a 'leisure centre', as amusement arcades are now referred to in up-market circles! Associated British Pathé had an office next door at 137 for several years and a couple of what are presumably cinema enthusiasts are studying the bill for *Stampede*. Supreme Cinemas had moved in by the early 1970s. The Argus shoe shop was at 135 for a long time, but is now derelict and the entire building is up for sale. In front of the trolleybus is the rear end of a Morris 10, while behind it is a two-door Morris 8 - with three-speed gearbox! *Photographer unknown*

Bottom This view of Royal Avenue was taken on 14 April 1968, looking towards North Street. BUT 219, proceeding towards Whitewell, is overtaking the tower wagon at the junction of Donegall Street, while the backs of a Daimler Fleetline, a Guy diesel bus and another trolleybus can be seen. The tower wagon (TW 56), later known as Recovery Vehicle 56, was scrapped in 1975. These wagons were designed in such a way that the platform could be placed under the wires while work was in progress, but when a trolleybus came along the platform was turned to be parallel to the direction of travel as in this picture; this meant that the wagon did not have to move each time a trolleybus arrived. The van behind the trolleybus is an Austin J type.

Duffin's menswear shop at the corner of Donegall Street has since disappeared and the entire block absorbed by the *Belfast Telegraph*. The block was known as 'Rea's Buildings' and was built about 1885. The three-storey building behind the trolleybus is the Belfast Public Library, built between 1883 and 1888 and still in daily use. For many years after the war it retained the scars made by German air gunners. *E. M. H. Humphreys*

Right This rear view of BUT 199 (GZ 8563) was taken in Donegall Square North on 29 March 1967. By this stage trolleybuses only used this set of overhead wires when going to Haymarket Depot. The motor bus visible ahead of the trolleybus is a Daimler Fleetline. By this date about 180 new double-deck buses had been placed in service as part of the trolleybus replacement programme.

On the extreme left is one of the recent bus stop signs complete with timetable panel, which were introduced in the city centre in the mid-1960s. On the second traction pole on the left can be seen an indicator box with two slots, one sloping to the left and one to the right. Whichever slot was illuminated indicated the way the overhead frog was set, the frog being activated by the handle located on the nearest traction pole, while the number of the frog was displayed by the sign 'P$_3$' above the indicator box. This number corresponded with the drivers' handbook of instructions for navigating the one-way scheme.

The large four-storey building to the right of the trolleybus is Imperial House

designed by Kendrick Evans in 1935 and somehow typifying 1930s architecture; it replaced the Linenhall Hotel. There are two Minis to the right of the trolleybus. *E. M. H. Humphreys*

Below Four years after the introduction of the one-way scheme around the City Hall, there is still a rather temporary air about the signs. The trolleybus on the right is bound for either Stormont or Dundonald via Albert Bridge, while that on the left is probably headed for Castlereagh.

The very ornate six-storey building at the corner of Donegall Square North and East was built by Young & Mackenzie for the Ocean Accident & Guarantee Corporation, and this is confirmed

by the sign below the level of the top storey. Originally known (not surprisingly) as Ocean House, it is currently called Pearl Assurance House after its present owners. Although somewhat modified at ground floor level, the building remains largely intact at the time of writing.

The church to the right of Imperial House was built in 1846-7 by Isaac Farrell for the Donegall Square Methodist congregation. It seated 1,500 worshippers and replaced a Methodist chapel on the site. Just over two years after its opening on 20 June 1847 it was destroyed by fire, but by 1850 it was completely rebuilt and survived until its closure in 1990; thankfully the facade was retained. *Denis Battams*

Top The main subject in this view of Donegall Square North is tram 359, a Chamberlain that entered service in 1930 and was 22 years old when Roy Brook took this photograph. In the background trolleybus 190 (GZ 8554), a BUT with GEC electrical equipment and Harkness 68-seater bodywork, which was new in 1950, is en route for Bloomfield via Albert Bridge. At that time trolleybuses on routes over the Albert Bridge came into town via Victoria Street and Chichester Street to the stand in Donegall Square East. They departed via May Street and Victoria Street and thence to the Albert Bridge. No 190 is on the overhead wires for Donegall Square East.

The trolley behind the tram appears to want to remain anonymous, but the number plate just visible to the right of the plinth, upon which Queen Victoria once proudly stood, shows it to be GZ 8572, from which the fleet number can be deduced as 208, also a BUT. Not all trolleybuses had the rear destination displays removed by the summer of 1952; the destination 'CROMAC SQUARE' suggests either that it is about to join the Ormeau route, or more likely to return to Haymarket Depot. A Bedford van is visible behind the tram, while a Hillman Minx is in the process of turning left into Donegall Square East.

The building with the clock was built in 1894 by Samuel Stevenson for Reuben Payne who was a merchant tailor in the early years of this century. Not surprisingly it became known as 'Payne's Buildings', although by 1953 it was occupied by James Pollock, photographic and audio dealer. Although altered on the ground floor, the building is still there today, albeit without the attractive conical roof. *Roy Brook*

Middle Guy 177 (GZ 8541) is captured on a wet day in 1951 while passing the Titanic Memorial outside the City Hall in Donegall Square North. The Memorial was erected in 1920, but moved to within the City Hall grounds I believe in the late 1950s, because of traffic congestion.

The trolleybus is destined for 'CARR'S GLEN VIA CLIFTONVILLE ROAD' and the additional 'VIA ALBERT BRIDGE' confirms that it has come from Cregagh, with which the route was linked. At the time this photograph was taken buses and trolleybuses retained the legend 'BELFAST CORPORATION' along their waistbands. The whisky advertising slogan 'Don't be vague - ask for Haig' was well known for very many years. The vehicle to the right of the trolleybus is an Austin A40 Pickup with trade plates, and two Austin taxis can just be discerned on either side of 177.

The four-storey building to the left of the trolleybus was the Water Office when this photograph was taken. It was built by Lanyon, Lynn and Lanyon as a warehouse for Richardson, Sons and Owden in 1867-69. Originally it had a magnificent Mansard roof, shown to good effect in Walker and Dixon's *No Mean City* of 1983, but the Blitz of 1941 destroyed it and it was replaced by a much more utilitarian structure. The building itself was beautifully restored by Marks & Spencer in 1985. *W. J. Wyse*

Bottom This rear view of Guy BTX 153 (GZ 8517) shows the rear destination display and 'BELFAST CORPORATION' legend along the waistband. Both of these features were discontinued in the early 1950s, so the picture was probably taken about 1952. The relatively bright '5' in the 153 on the back suggests that a new stock of transfers has been recently delivered!

No 153 is at the Carr's Glen stop in Donegall Square North, with the City Hall on the left and the Scottish Provident Institution building on the right of the picture. The advertisement for the CWS (Co-Operative Wholesale Society) on the side of the bus reflected a time when the 'Co-Op' movement was strong in Belfast and other working cities. Essentially the idea was that the Co-Op would provide everything a family needed in the way of groceries, butcher's meat, chemist supplies, coal, milk and drapery, and in return for loyal custom it would give a dividend on everything purchased (usually a shilling in the pound, or 5 per cent). To do this every customer would be allocated a share number (my mother's

was 52664 - still remembered 40 years later!), and this would be quoted at the time of purchase. Four times a year - the 'Co Quarter' - the dividend would be entered in the 'Share Book' from which it could be withdrawn, lodged to savings or used to buy any goods or services from 'The Co'. In Belfast the top floor of the Co-Op building in York Street was where all these records were maintained and where withdrawals could be made.

A further advantage was the credit system, which allowed working people to obtain goods on credit provided the amount was settled by the date of the 'Co Quarter'. Eventually the Co-operative movement grew to include farms, funeral parlours, canning plants, florists and dairies. *Photographer unknown, courtesy of David Harvey*

Right Guy BTX 113 (FZ 7898) is standing at the Bloomfield stop outside Robinson & Cleaver's department store in Donegall Square North in the early 1960s. Its trolleys are on the innermost pair of wires for Bloomfield - the centre set is for Cregagh trolleybuses while the outer set leads into the Dundonald and Stormont layby on Chichester Street.

Gilpin Brothers' store on the opposite corner of Donegall Place was a three-storey building erected about 1870 on the site of the Royal Hotel. Linenhall Chambers, which accommodated Gilpins, was replaced by Donegall House in 1968, and the ground floor is currently occupied by a branch of H. Samuel, the jeweller.

Robinson & Cleaver's store, to the right of the trolleybus, was opened in 1888. Reaching six storeys, it was built in an Italianate style by Young and Mackenzie and included many innovations such as electric light and a 'luxurious passenger elevator'. The interior was dominated by a 'nobly proportioned and exceedingly beautiful staircase of white Sicilian marble'. Regretfully the firm ceased trading in the 1980s, but the building was converted to individual shops and offices, including a Burger King restaurant, and the preservation of the facade has been carried out with great success. *Robert Mack*

Below No 164 (GZ 8528), a Guy BTX, is at the Dundonald via Queen's Bridge stand in Chichester Street in September 1957. Before the City Hall one-way scheme was introduced in July 1958, all Queen's Bridge trolleybuses (ie the Dundonald, Stormont and Castlereagh routes) left from Chichester Street, while all the Albert Bridge vehicles departed from the stand in Donegall Square East.

The motor bus heading for Cherryvalley on route 76 is ex-London Daimler CWA6 506 (GYE 65). Initially it had been fitted with a Brush 56-seater utility body for service in London, and ran for some months with its original body in Belfast; it was later rebodied by Harkness. It carries the familiar advertisement 'Guinness is good for you', while the rather more mundane one on the trolleybus refers to 'Paint Shops & Stores Ltd' of Kent Street. The Kent Street site was demolished some time ago and served as a car park; there is no listing of the firm in the current Northern Ireland phone book, so it may no longer be in business.

The buildings behind the trolleybuses, although having been altered at ground floor level, are still easily recognisable today. The blind firmly pulled down on the 'Sports House' confirms that the photograph was taken on a Sunday. *Denis Battams*

Top This view of AEC 98 (FZ 7883) was taken on Saturday 30 March 1963 on the occasion of the commemoration of the end of trolleybus operation to Stormont and Dundonald. A special tour was organised by the Northern Ireland Road and Rail Development Association to mark both this event and that of Belfast Trolleybuses' Silver Jubilee - the first trolleybus operated on 28 March 1938.

I certainly recognise many faces here, including John Laird, Derek Young and - provider of a number of photographs used in this book - Richard Whitford. I am sorry to say that several other enthusiasts have passed away in the intervening period of more than 30 years. The location of the photograph is the Stormont trolleybus stop in Chichester Street. *Photographer unknown*

Middle Taken by Denis Battams on 9 September 1957 before the introduction of the City Hall one-way scheme the following July, this photograph illustrates several modifications that had been made to Fleet Number 1 (EZ 7889) since its entry into service almost 20 years before (a view of No 1 in its early days can be seen on page 81). The route number box has been moved from the nearside to the offside, mainly to make it much more convenient for the driver to change the display. The livery has been changed from blue to red and the lining out has become much more utilitarian.

For a period Jordan's, to the right of the trolleybus, was a branch of the Halifax Building Society. The two smaller three-storey buildings directly behind No 1 were built in the late 19th century. One of the shops that occupied the ground floor in the early 1950s, known as Campbell's Patisserie, had its name in Egyptian-style lettering at varying angles to the perpendicular. At that time I was just learning 'joined-up writing' and can clearly remember wondering what on earth my teacher would say about such untidy letters! The large three-storey building was the Belfast Bank, and its facade has been preserved by its new owners, the Halifax Building Society.

The bus on the left, 471 (GYE 56), was one of 100 purchased from London Transport in 1953 to expedite tram replacement; this example was rebodied by Harkness in 1954. *Denis Battams*

Bottom The same scene taken on 30 March 1996. Guy 112 (FZ 7897) has been restored by the Ulster Folk & Transport Museum into whose care it was given in 1968. Although the trolley wires were removed almost 30 years ago, 112 is capable once again of operating under power.

No 2667 (VXI 2667) is a Leyland Tiger with a locally built 51-seater Alexander body (it can also accommodate 22 standing passengers); it first entered service with Citybus in 1991. It is interesting to note that the trolleybus, with 68 seats and room for a further 5 standees, had the same passenger-carrying capacity as the modern single-decker!

No 3000 (DAZ 3000) is a Volvo B10M with a Van Hool body that can accommodate 79 seated passengers and a further 21 standees. It first went into service with Citybus in 1994, principally on the City Express services beyond Glengormley. Its articulation gives it a surprising amount of flexibility in service.

The former Belfast Bank building with ground floor pillars and roof balustrade has been cleaned up and looks very well. The three-storey building in red sandstone has been demolished and replaced by offices for the Belfast (now Northern) Bank, the Bank of Ireland, the Irish Permanent Building Society and H. Samuel, the jeweller - the change has perhaps not been for the better. *Ulster Folk & Transport Museum*

This view of Guy 177 (GZ 8541) and BUT 191 (GZ 8555) in Donegall Square North shows clearly how outwardly similar the two classes of trolleybus appeared. Both had GEC electrical equipment and 68-seater double-deck bodies by the Belfast firm of Harkness. No 177 is bound for Whitewell – by the time this photograph was taken, in August 1962, the Whitehouse route had been closed for several months. No 191 is headed for Carr's Glen and has just come from Cregagh (as suggested by the display in the 'via' box). The bus behind, 456 (GLX 904), was originally fitted with a Duple 56-seater body and was bought from London Transport as part of a batch of 100 in 1953. It was one of 18 vehicles to receive a new 56-seater Harkness body before going into service in Belfast; the remainder entered service with their original bodies and were withdrawn and rebodied in groups.

Just visible behind 456 is the scaffolding surrounding the erection of the new offices for the Prudential Assurance Company. The car to the left of 177 is unmistakably an Austin, complete with the older style of AA badge, while a couple of Morris Minors and a Volkswagen van can be seen further back. *Denis Battams*

Above By the time that this photograph was taken, perhaps about 1960, the two three-storey buildings to the right of the Belfast Bank in Donegall Square North had been demolished to make way for Bank House, the new Central Branch of the Belfast Banking Company. The Ulster Architectural Heritage Society in its excellent work *Central Belfast* describes the building as 'a five-storey office block with panels of Portland stone flanking a central curtain walled section, with recessed entrance and attic floor slightly set back; a demonstration that prestigious materials do not necessarily make a fine office'. The buildings that attracted this comment can be seen on page 33.

The trolleybus, Guy BTX 143 (GZ 8507) with GEC electrical equipment and Harkness 68-seater bodywork, is headed for Cregagh via Albert Bridge. The motor bus, 318 (MZ 7416), is also a Guy with Harkness 54-seater bodywork, demonstrating the significant difference in car-

rying capacity between the two modes of transport at that time. The bus is on its way to 'LM&S RAILWAY', which at that time was linked with Springfield Road, hence the indication on the lower blind 'VIA GROSVENOR ROAD'. The advertisement for milk on the trolleybus compares with that for Booth's gin on the bus!
Photographer unknown

Above right Sunbeam semi-utility trolleybus 142 (GZ 2813) is boarding passengers at the Falls Road stop in Donegall Square North in 1951. A horse and cart are parked inconveniently outside the Scotch Wool and Hosiery Store and a private car is parked nearby. AEC 83 (FZ 7868) is about to overtake 142 on its way to Greencastle a few months after the opening of the route. Because of a dispute with the Ulster Transport Authority (UTA), BCT vehicles did not convey passengers beyond Whitehouse Post Office, although trolleybuses had to go to Whitehouse turning circle to turn. Older trolleybuses showed 'GREENCASTLE' on their destination blinds, while later ones used 'WHITEHOUSE'. However,

both destination displays referred to the same turning circle at Merville Garden Village.

To the right of the trolleybus is the Linenhall Library, as the Belfast Society for Promoting Knowledge is better known. Although it began life in Ann Street, at the beginning of the 19th century it moved to the White Linen Hall from which it took its nickname. When that building was demolished in 1898 to make way for the City Hall, it moved to its present site. The official title is proudly displayed at the entrance.

The building directly behind 83 is Prudential Chambers, which was built by Young and Mackenzie in 1913. The three buildings further up Wellington Place were originally part of a terrace of houses. The large building at the corner of Queen Street housed the Athletic Stores, which, despite several terrorist bombs, traded until fairly recently; the building was demolished and replaced by Sun Alliance House in 1985-86. Beyond Queen Street the three-storey brick building housed the Liverpool & London & Globe Insurance Company. *Alan B. Cross*

Left Guy 157 (GZ 8521) is waiting for passengers to board in Victoria Square, probably in the late 1940s, given that the route numbers changed in February 1951. At that time and until the introduction of the City Hall one-way system in July 1958, this was the rather inconveniently located city centre terminus of the Ormeau Road service, part of a general 'ban the bus from the city centre' phase that many local authorities went through just after the war. It was not a popular decision and no further routes were treated in this cavalier way!

An old-style telephone kiosk can be seen in silhouette; this has since been replaced with a modern British Telecom example. The white band painted on the traction pole indicates a manually operated frog on the overhead line. Normally set to the right, the turning circle could be used in either direction, for example to reverse trolleybuses from East Belfast during the Twelfth of July parades.

The building in the background was erected in about 1875 for Cantrell & Cochrane, mineral water manufacturers, who had a well in Victoria Square. It has since been demolished and the site is now occupied by the Victoria Centre, a modern shopping mall. The building on the right nearest the trolleybus has been demolished to make way for Churchill House, the major British Telecom office in the city, but apart from superficial changes to the ground floor the five-storey building nearest the camera is still intact. *Photographer unknown*

Below Seen in almost the same location as the previous photograph, BUT 226 (OZ 7328) waits at the Ormeau Road stand beside the building constructed by W. J. Gilliland in 1893 for T. & J. McErval, seed merchants. At the time of writing this building is still standing, but changes to the ground floor include number 38's conversion to Discount Travel, while the shop to the right has become Ginger Snaps ladies' hairdresser. *Robert Mack*

Above Guy BTX 148 (GZ 8512) is seen on Donegall Quay on Saturday 11 August 1962 while heading for Holywood Arches via Queen's Bridge. By this date there was still a 12-minute timetabled service on Saturdays to Connswater (Holywood Arches) via Queen's Bridge, plus a further 12-minutes service to Knock Road. Both of these were in addition to the 'regular' 12-minutes service to the terminus at Dundonald. There was also a substantial service to both Knock Road and Dundonald via Albert Bridge!

The CWS logo encouraged shoppers to 'Shop at the Co-Op' - at that time 'The Co' was still a major player in the grocery business. The building behind and to the left of the trolleybus is the Custom House, opened in 1857; it is credited to Charles Lanyon. Fortunately it is still there today, although currently undergoing substantial internal refurbishment.

'The Sheds' for Glasgow, Ardrossan, Heysham and Liverpool vessels were to the right. Until the arrival of roll-on/roll-off ferries and the increasing popularity of air travel, this area was a hive of activity each evening as the steamers prepared to leave for the overnight sailings to the mainland. For many years after the war hundreds of people queued outside the British Railways office in Donegall Place on a particular day in February when the sailing tickets for the Heysham boat went on sale for the 'Twelfth' holiday period. None of 'The Sheds' remain today; the entire area is currently under redevelopment, with new road and rail bridges over the River Lagan and a new bus station being built on the city side of Donegall Quay. *Denis Battams*

Above Guy 117 (FZ 7902) was photographed a little further along Donegall Quay in the direction of the Queen's Bridge. Making for Castlereagh, it is just passing the Ardrossan shed. Until its closure there was a railway line along Donegall Quay, which connected the Belfast Central Railway with the Belfast & Northern Counties at York Road, but it had not provided a passenger service for many years before this photograph was taken in the 1960s. The track was located just behind the wall. *Robert Mack*

Above Donegall Quay was almost deserted when Richard Whitford took this view of Guy GZ 8552 on 11 September 1962. I often wonder why the word 'STORMONT' was added to the phrase 'PARLIAMENT BUILDINGS'; 'STORMONT' by itself was used to indicate vehicles that turned at Stormont gates.

James Glennon's sack and bag shop and the hotel next door have been demolished, as indeed has the modern mill owned by J. T. Green just to the left of the trolleybus. At present a new bus station and car park are being built on the site. The two vans in the picture are an Austin A35 outside the former Ulster Temperance hotel, and a Ford 15 cwt van. *Richard Whitford*

Below Just preparing to turn left from Donegall Quay on to Queen's Bridge, Guy 157 (GZ 8521) is en route to Dundonald. Unfortunately the date is not known, but from the evidence I would estimate it to be about 1960. With the exception of Tedford's ships chandlers shop, all the buildings in the background have been demolished. In 1992 a new office block was built upon the site of The Red Dragon public house on the corner; it now dwarfs Tedford's building. Tedford's initially began trading in Donaghadee in 1851 and moved to Donegall Quay in 1855. James Tedford diversified into ship-owning in the days when his vessels were able to moor outside his front door! Although the business closed in 1991, it has since re-opened under new management. The three-wheel pulley block hanging at first floor level has been a symbol of the company for many years. *Colin Routh*

Right As already mentioned, 'de-wire-ments' were relatively rare in Belfast, and this one in Ann Street appears to have been caused by Guy 127 (FZ 7912) having attempted to pass the road works while its trolleys were on the wires nearest the kerb. It is possible that this was in error, as the inner wires turned left into Victoria Street in the direction of May Street and vehicles on the 31 route would have turned right at the Victoria Street junction using the centre wires, which led to High Street. The outer wires kept to the right-hand side of Ann Street and Victoria Street and turned right into Queen's Square, joining those leading to the Queen's Bridge. This arrangement allowed trolleybuses to use the loop as a terminus, usually displaying 'ALBERT MEMORIAL' on these (relatively unusual) journeys; in fact, 'ALBERT MEMORIAL' can just be discerned above 'HOUSTON PARK' on the destination indicator of the front vehicle.

Behind, No 143 (GZ 8507), returning from Castlereagh, was one of 70 Guy BTXs with GEC electrical equipment and Harkness 68-seater bodies to be delivered to Belfast between 1947 and 1950. This particular vehicle entered service in 1948.

A. J. Stuart's hardware business has since been replaced by Russell House - since this is where fixed penalty parking tickets are paid, it is probably one of the least popular offices in Belfast! Beyond it, the red-brick four-storey building, built about 1880, currently houses 'Paddy's Bar', while more recent buildings nearer the river accommodate Elliott's Hire Company. The Belfast Transport Social Club was located here and, in addition to our own Royal Navy, by all accounts played host to those of the Free French, Dutch and Polish during the war. On the right the large building to the east of Musgrave Street is still there, but the sin-gle-storey temporary erection and the four-storey block, known as Queen Anne Buildings, beside the black and white striped traction pole was cleared away in 1989 to make way for the Musgrave Street Police Station extension and car park. The original site for the Belfast Central Railway terminus was planned for the corner of Ann Street and Victoria Street. On the left is a Morris and on the right a Wolseley. *Denis Battams*

Right AEC 56 (FZ 7841) passes the Law Courts while en route to Cregagh in the early 1960s. This impressive building was constructed between 1928 and 1933 by James G. West of London, and was to become the target of many bomb attacks during the 1970s and '80s. Following restoration, permanent security mea-sures have included the construction of a new boundary wall to Oxford Street and a neo-classical sentry box on Victoria Street. The small wall behind the vehicles has been strengthened against terrorist attack by the addition of a metal screen 10 feet (3 metres) high. On the left is a Wolseley (OZ 2366), parked in the background is a Ford Anglia (TZ 275), and a Ford Zephyr with a 'VZ' registration pokes in on the right. The man on the bike glimpsed behind the

'KEEP LEFT' sign is riding a moped - fairly uncommon today, these were motor cycles that could also be pedalled up hills, since the engines in those days were not very powerful! *Colin Routh, courtesy of Andrew Bronn*

Left AEC 96 (FZ 7881) is seen in Oxford Street on 11 August 1962, just over a year before the Cregagh route became bus-operated. No 96 had GEC electrical equipment and, in common with almost all Belfast trolleybuses, Harkness 68-seater bodywork. The unpainted waist panel on the nearside is clearly seen, and below it the pole used to retrieve de-wired trolley booms, the hook being near the front. It was the damage caused to the panel by the metal hook that gave rise to the decision not to paint it. While this was understandable, it did nothing for the appearance of the trolleybus.

The start of the wires for the long siding for Haymarket Depot can be clearly seen, with the back of the indicator box just visible behind the first traction pole on the right. This box had two sets of lights angled left and right; whichever was illuminated indicated the direction in which the frog was set.

St George's Market is on the left, the Royal Courts of Justice is in the middle background, and the two-storey red-brick building beyond was the Headquarters of the Belfast Fire Brigade. The Brigade moved to new premises in Ormeau Avenue in 1993, partly due to difficulties experienced in getting fire engines in and out because of security precautions around the Law Courts. At the time of writing all three buildings are still standing. Parked outside the market are two Ford Anglia vans and an Anglia saloon, while behind the trolleybus is a Volkswagen 'Beetle'. *Denis Battams*

Below left Guy 168 (GZ 8532) is turning left from Oxford Street into East Bridge Street on the Cregagh route in the early 1960s. This particular trolleybus is today one of five preserved vehicles, the others being 98, 112, 183 and 246; it was donated to the National Trolleybus Association upon its retirement in 1968.

The two sets of wires at this point was an attempt to overcome the problem of trolleybuses bound for Haymarket Depot blocking through vehicles. Initially there was a right-hand turn from East Bridge Street into Stewart Street, but trolleybuses waiting to cross the line of traffic heading into town blocked service vehicles making for the Albert Bridge. The introduction of the long lead into the right-hand turn therefore allowed depot-bound buses to wait near the centre of the roadway, permitting the service vehicles to pass them on the inside.

St George's Market can again be seen on the left, designed by J. C. Bretland, the City Surveyor, and built in stages between 1890 and 1896. Market traders still operate from here (just), but this is the last market from which the area takes its name. The wall on the right surrounded the Aberdeen Market, which was previously known as the Cattle Market, the Pork market and May's Market. It has since been demolished and development of the Laganside concert hall has just begun. The van on the left of the picture is an Austin J type, and behind it is a Ford Zephyr and a Morris Minor. *Robert Mack*

Above right Guy 181 (GZ 8545) is in East Bridge Street on 6 June 1953 en route to Rosetta, an intermediate terminus on the Ormeau route, with an unidentified trolleybus on the Bloomfield route in the background. The wires under which 181 is working crossed to the left-hand side of East Bridge Street and turned left into Cromac Street and thence to the Ormeau Road. The tram track and overhead wires are still evident, as even at this stage the trams using Mountpottinger Depot went via Albert Bridge. The difficulty of managing tram and trolleybus overhead is evident in the

'dog's hind leg' route of the tram wire. Fortunately there was a great deal of lateral tolerance in both the tram and the trolleybus system of current collection.

To the right is Annette Street from which a pair of trolleybus wires can just be seen emerging; this was the route most often used by trolleybuses entering service from Haymarket Depot. The pub on the corner was the Royal George, later known as James McGlennon's. The bus stop on the right was for all routes except Ormeau Road, the main reason being that Ormeau Road trolleybuses could pass vehicles going into town.

The building behind 118 was the City of Liverpool Hide, Skin and Fat Co. When asked why a Liverpool Company chose to base itself in this part of Belfast, one answer was that the smell that emerged from their works was such that Liverpudlians demanded that it be located as far away from their area as possible! The twin towers in the left background belonged to the Corporation Electricity Department's generating station, which was originally developed to supply power for the electric trams. The car on the left is a pre-war Morris, while the open van on the right is a battery-operated float belonging to New City Minerals. In the 1950s and '60s several firms in Belfast delivered minerals to the door, and often operated battery-powered vehicles in the tightly knit network of streets, finding that this was the most economical method of delivery.

The entire area has now been demolished and Annette Street has been built over by Friendly Street, from which several distinctly unfriendly terrorist attacks have been launched over the years! *John Price*

Above There are relatively few photographs of this batch of trolley-buses, partly because they were all retired by 1960. No 141 (GZ 2812) was a Sunbeam W semi-utility vehicle that entered service in 1946. It was fitted with BTH electrical equipment and a 56-seater Harkness body, but unusually for Belfast it had only four wheels. This was its most distinctive feature for trolleybus-spotters, although aficionados will also note the rather angular finish to the roof.

The photograph was taken in Donegall Square East in September 1957. Although showing route number 24, this number was never used by trolleybuses, and 141 is coming off service, headed for Short Strand Depot. The route number for Stormont via Albert Bridge was 23, and it is possible that the driver simply turned up 24 rather than wind the blind the whole way back to a blank - the 'official' way. Early destination displays showed 'SHORT STRAND [ALBERT BRIDGE]' on the top blind, often supplemented by 'VIA ALBERT BRIDGE' on the bottom blind. Trolleybuses bound for Short Strand via Queen's Bridge displayed 'BRIDGE END' (which may just be discerned as the next display on the top blind).

Pollocks, in the background, is now the Bradford & Bingley Building Society, and has regrettably lost its very attractive conical roof. On the right Ocean Buildings is still there, although the Commercial Cable Company has given way to the Cheltenham & Gloucester Building Society, and the building has been renamed 'Pearl Assurance House'. The bus whose bonnet is just visible on the left is a Guy, while heading towards Chichester Street is a Morris 8. A Karrier Bantam lorry is coming into Donegall Square East and a Hillman Minx is parked outside Ocean Buildings. *Denis Battams*

Below It is difficult to date this view taken by John Parke also in Donegall Square East. Given that 135 is on the Bloomfield route, which did not open until 1946, and that the 'figure 8' loop had not been installed on the overhead wiring, I would think that the late 1940s would be as close as it is possible to come. No 135 (GZ 2806) was one of the same semi-utility batch as 141 above, but No 2 behind it (FZ 7890) was an AEC with English Electric electrical equipment and Harkness 68-seater bodywork. It is still painted in the 'swept down' style of streamlining so popular in the 1930s, and its 'via' blind is incorrectly set, as by this date outward journeys to Cregagh were routed via May Street. *John Parke*

Right This view shows one of the original group of 14 experimental trolleybuses, 12 (EZ 7900), a Leyland TTB with GEC electrical equipment and Leyland 68-seater bodywork. Originally painted in the streamlining of the period (see opposite), it has been repainted in the standard blue livery of the immediate post-war era; the beading that was used as a guideline for the 'swept down' look of the early days is still visible on the upper and lower deck panels.

The Albert Bridge routes had been diverted into Donegall Square East, where this view was taken, in 1944, and from the available evidence I would date the photograph in the early 1950s. Stormont and Dundonald trolleybuses shared the same barrier, as indicated by the rather crude sign on the traction pole, as did the Bloomfield and Cregagh services. By the time this photograph was taken the 'figure 8' overhead wiring loop was in place, allowing vehicles to enter and leave the stands independently. Later a further bypass wire was added to allow vehicles to pass straight through.
Photographer unknown

Below The occasion of this photograph was inevitably a sad one for everybody present. The group had assembled to make one of the last trips on a Belfast trolleybus as part of the official 'Last Trolleybus' tributes. The day is Saturday 11 May 1968 (the day before the actual last day, as Belfast Corporation would not hold a formal civic function on the Sabbath in those days). Guys 112 (FZ 7897) and 168 (8532) are preceded by Sunbeam 246 (2206 OI), which incidentally was the only trolley-bus in Belfast to receive a registration number with the letters and numbers reversed. The official party had not yet arrived and in order to facilitate normal Saturday traffic the trolleybuses were parked on the 'wrong' side of the road. Following the introduction of the City Hall one-way scheme in 1958, Donegall Square East was no longer used for trolleybus stands, and motor buses for routes in South Belfast left from there. *E. M. H. Humphreys*

Above By contrast, this view was taken at the site of the ceremony to mark the introduction of trolleybuses to Belfast, and shows 197 (GZ 8561) - a BUT 9641T - turning left from Castle Street into Queen Street. Lipton's shop on the extreme left is now a J. & J. Foods store, but the Hercules Bar is still there. It was built about 1865 and took its name from Hercules Street, in which there were many butcher shops; it was replaced by Royal Avenue in 1884. The LMW is now Eastwood's bookmakers. *E. M. H. Humphreys*

Below Guy 150 (GZ 8514) was in Queen Street when this photograph was taken in about the mid-1960s. As many of the vehicles on the Falls Road routes operated only to the city centre, rather than going through to Whitewell, they used the Queen Street/Wellington Place/Donegall Place/Castle Street loop established at the start of trolleybus operation in 1938. The advertisement for Guinness may be rather dated and its strength-enhancing claim may not pass the rigorous tests of today's Trades Description Act, but the product is as popular as ever!

Today the restaurant beside the bus is a model shop, and the two units to the right comprise Romano's restaurant. 'Leisureworld' is now located to the right of the four-storey building at the extreme left of the picture. The black car behind the trolleybus is a Ford Anglia 105E, while the bus is passing a Mini. *Robin Symons*

Above This view of Guy 172 (GZ 8536) emerging from Queen Street and about to turn left into Wellington Place was taken on 15 June 1964. The bus is on a Falls Road to Whitewell cross-town service and is heading to the Whitewell stand in Wellington Place.

The seven-storey building on the right was a warehouse originally built for Alex King the coal merchant, and imaginatively named 'Kingscourt'. It was later used by the Athletic Stores as a sports department store, as seen here, until replaced by Sun Alliance House in 1986.

The half-constructed building to the left is the new offices for the Royal Insurance Group on which is unofficially being advertised 'PTQ', the Queen's University Student Rag magazine ('PTQ' stands for 'Pro Tanto Quid', the first three words of Belfast's motto, which, part of the city's coat-of-arms, was carried by every Belfast Corporation Transport Department vehicle). The four-storey warehouse next door was built in 1911 by Watt, Tulloch and Fitzsimmons and today houses the Educational Company, the Athletic Stores, and the Arrow Insurance Office, amongst others. The single-storey white building in the far background is now the 147 Snooker Club. All the buildings beyond the Athletic Stores visible on the right-hand side of Queen Street have been demolished and replaced by the new Fountain shopping centre. On the left can be seen a Mini, an Austin and two 1100s, while there is yet another Morris Minor leading 172 into Wellington Place. *John Gillham*

Above right Guy 127 (FZ 7812) is on the 'inner' pair of wires in Castle Street on 12 April 1966 with the crew taking a break.

Behind is the newest trolleybus in Belfast (and destined to be the last), Sunbeam 246 (2206 OI) on the 'outer' wires.

The building to the left was the Bank Buildings and that to the right Anderson & McAuley's. Both were 'up-market' department stores, and although both have ceased trading in their original way, the buildings still stand - Bank Buildings now trades as Primark while Anderson & McAuley houses Habitat on the ground floor. Barnett & Hutton, in the background on the far side of Donegall Place, is now a McDonald's. Sawer's shop and the Norwich Union building on the right replaced the bomb site that had lain derelict for many years. *E. M. H. Humphreys*

Left Semi-utility Sunbeam W 135 (GZ 2806) is at the Falls Road stand in Castle Street in the early 1950s, about to depart on a short working to Falls Park. These wartime vehicles were significantly smaller than the Belfast standard, having only 56 seats instead of the more usual 68, and as such required only a four-wheeled chassis. This particular vehicle, although built to semi-utility specifications, for example having an angular roof as compared to the vehicle immediately behind, was delivered in 1946 and lasted in service until 1960. The area behind the trolleybus was the derelict bomb site referred to in the previous caption. *Roy Marshall*

Below This is a typical view of a busy Castle Street in the late 1950s before the redevelopers (official and unofficial) rendered the left-hand side barely recognisable today. AEC 97 is making its way to Glen Road having crossed the town from either Whitehouse or Whitewell; the route number blind, although correctly displayed, has become rather twisted. The overhead wiring was still carried on gantries as opposed to the later span wires. Essentially this method of construction used existing tramway traction poles, the tubular cross-bars substantially enhancing their strength.

Hughes fruit shop on the extreme left has disappeared, as has the tobacconist next door, to be replaced by a modernised newsagent; the enamel signs all advertised Wills's tobacco products, some long gone. The Great Eastern pub is now a branch of Winemark, but the right-hand side of Castle Street remains easily recognisable.

The owner of the Morris estate car outside the tobacconists looks as if he is about to be booked for parking illegally. The car in front is a Ford Anglia, while that parked on the right is a Sunbeam Talbot. *C. Carter*

BELFAST TROLLEYBUSES 1938-1968

Right The Belfast Banking Company on the left of Waring Street was built as the Assembly Rooms in 1769, making it one of the oldest public buildings in Belfast. It was built by Robert Taylor in 1776, converted to a bank by Sir Charles Lanyon in 1845, and refurbished and extended several times. The company was taken over by the Northern Bank some years ago, but the exterior of the building is virtually unchanged from this photograph. The building just in front of the trolleybus was built by Thomas Jackson & Son between 1867 and 1872; it was occupied by McCalla Travel when the photograph was taken on 15 June 1964, and later became the Cornerhouse Restaurant. It is currently empty. The Commercial Buildings on the right were erected by John McCutcheon between 1819 and 1822, although the date panel reads 'MDCCCXX', which Latin scholars will immediately identify as 1820! Its initial purpose was to provide 'an excellent commercial hotel, a spacious and handsome newsroom and a piazza for the use of merchants'. It was occupied for many years by the *Northern Whig* newspaper, but regretfully has lain vacant for some time. The cars visible in the photograph include a Ford Consul and an Austin A40. *John Gillham*

Below Another rear view, this time of Guy BTX 120 (FZ 7905) in Lower Donegall Street on the same day in 1964. Since 120 has taken the inner wires, it will go up Clifton Street either to the Antrim Road/Glengormley or to Carr's Glen. The circular advertisement on the corner of the bus is for Robertson's jam; in those days there was less concern about the political correctness that gave rise to the recent controversy surrounding the company's use of the 'golliwog' symbol.

Cathedral Buildings to the left of the picture was built around the turn of the century on the site of the Fourth Presbyterian Meeting House. Outside are parked a Wolseley 4/44 and an Austin, and there is a Standard at the traffic lights. On the other side is a Ford Zephyr and behind it a Volkswagen van. The building at the corner of Royal Avenue and Lower Donegall Street was occupied by the Ulster Carpet Centre, but was replaced by Mark Royal House shortly after this photograph was taken. Duffin's men's shop across Royal Avenue has since been demolished to make way for the increased accommodation needs of the *Belfast Telegraph*.

The *Irish News* office near the centre of the picture is still there, though missing its gable advertisement, while Woodhouse's, built in the mid-1930s, and occupied by a succession of cheap furniture outlets, is currently hoping for a tenant. The car park just visible to the right is now the grounds of the University of Ulster at Belfast (formerly the College of Art and Design). *John Gillham*

The final view of the city centre is of Guy BTX 107 (FZ 7892), well-laden en route to Bellevue on 11 August 1962. By this time all trolleybuses had been fitted with flashing indicator lights, which were considerably more effective than the semaphore trafficators they replaced. St Anne's Cathedral, behind the trolleybus, was built between 1898 and 1904 by Thomas Drew. The west front was added in 1925-27, while south and north transepts were built between 1964 and 1981. *Denis Battams*

EAST BELFAST

THIS SECTION covers the area from Belfast Lough to Cregagh Road. In many ways East Belfast was the home of trolleybuses; although the first route to be established was Falls Road in West Belfast, from 1942 to 1946 all new trolleybus routes were in the east of the city. Clough Smith erected all the overhead as a single contract, although the rate at which routes were converted from trams to trolleybuses was governed mainly by the rate at which new trolleybuses could be delivered.

Cregagh was the first route to open and a temporary depot was established in the Hay Market (two words) near East Bridge Street. It was quickly followed by Castlereagh, Dundonald and Stormont. Bloomfield opened after the war in 1946 and the short-lived Holywood Road followed in 1952.

There were a number of impressive junctions, notably Albert Bridge and Short Strand, Queen's Bridge and Short Strand, Mountpottinger Road and Albertbridge Road, and Ropeworks corner (sometimes known as 'Ben-Ell' corner). Before 1963 most of the routes were worked by trolleybuses, the only exceptions being Cherryvalley and Sydenham. The two major running depots were located in East Belfast at Haymarket (one word) and Short Strand.

Although the destination screen of 105 (FZ 7890) shows 'CASTLEREAGH', in fact it is heading across Queen's Bridge towards the city centre - either it has been turned too soon or too late! McCreary tram 423 is bound for the County Down Railway Station, although it is incorrectly displaying '57' in its route number box!

In 1953, when this photograph was taken, a number of cross-channel ships moored at Donegall Quay and there were many cranes along the quayside like the one shown here on the right. As a child I was fascinated by the crane's two short legs, which ran on a rail mounted near the roof of the sheds, and the two long legs that used a rail on the quay itself. Queen's Bridge lost its street lights in the Blitz; they had been mounted on elegant pillars, which had been set into concrete plinths adorned with the city's coat-of-arms. They have now been beautifully restored. *J. H. Price*

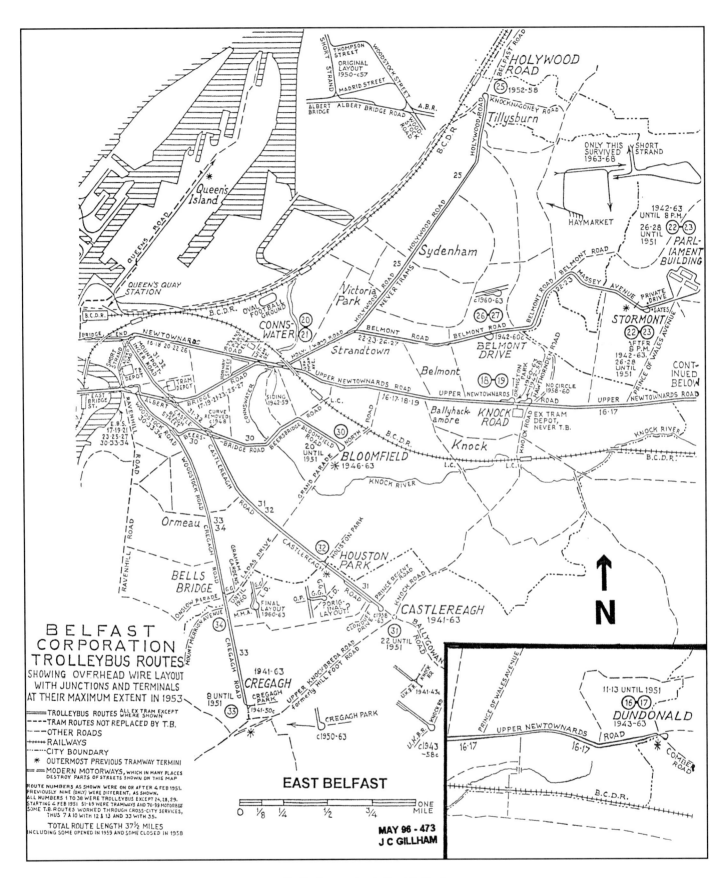

Trolleybus routes in East Belfast.

No 168 (GZ 8522) is in Bridge End, looking towards the city centre, in 1962. The railway bridge in the distance was originally built to link the Belfast Central Railway with the Belfast & County Down, whose terminus was on the 'wrong' side of the River Lagan.

Shortly after this photograph was taken the bridge was demolished as part of the new Queen Elizabeth II Bridge works (or so it was claimed). However, the rejuvenation of Northern Ireland Railways, the opening of Belfast Central station and the re-inte-

gration of the Bangor line into the network required the bridge to be re-installed! The bridge is about the only feature in this photograph still standing; all the other buildings were swept away to make way for the new approaches to the Sydenham Bypass. Indeed, in February 1996 the changes to the area are so marked that it is difficult to identify reference points between the photographs. The two main ones are the left-hand kerb-line in the centre of the pictures and the railway bridge. *Richard Whitford/ Mike Maybin*

Left Guy 117 (FZ 7902) was photographed at Bridge End near the junction with Short Strand, probably in the early 1960s, about to turn right up Mountpottinger Road on its way to Castlereagh. The network of overhead wires at the junction was quite considerable, and allowed trolleybuses to go from Bridge End to Newtownards Road, Mountpottinger Road and Short Strand. Additionally there was the facility for depot trolleybuses to operate from Short Strand to and from Newtownards Road.

Park Drive cigarettes, advertised on the side of the trolleybus, were made by Gallaher's of York Street. At best they were regarded as 'economical' - at about the same level as Woodbines. In my youth they could be bought singly (I am told), and it was the epitome of sophistication to be seen smoking a Park Drive, or, if things were really bad, a Woodbine! The horse appears to be pulling a very heavy load, although the driver does not seem to think of helping by getting off and walking. Again, all the buildings in the picture were demolished about 30 years ago to make way for the Sydenham Bypass. *Andrew Bronn*

Below Another view of the complex overhead junction at Bridge End, this time looking east on 31 January 1962, just a year or so before the main East Belfast routes were converted to motor buses. Guy 153 (GZ 8517) carries the route number '18', indicating that it is returning from Knock Road, a short working of the Dundonald service. The junction has since been extensively re-aligned and is unrecognisable today, forming part of a new approach to the Sydenham Bypass, which is just visible in the centre background. There are three Morris Minors discernible in the picture! *Richard Whitford*

Above This photograph was taken in Grampian Avenue in September 1962, looking towards the Upper Newtownards Road. Guy 152 (GZ 8516) is on a relatively unusual short working known as 'Holywood Arches', which operated mainly on Saturday afternoons in the late 1950s and early '60s primarily for the inner suburban shoppers of the Connswater area. The trolleybuses followed the usual Dundonald route as far as Connswater bridge and Upper Newtownards Road, then turned left into Grampian Avenue and left again into Holywood Road, allowing passengers to board at the stop near Grampian Street.

In the left background is Bloomfield Baptist Church, which together with the houses on the left-hand side of the street is easily recognisable today. By the left-hand kerb is yet another Morris Minor, with an Austin, a Standard and a Ford further up the street; on the right is a Ford Anglia. *Richard Whitford*

Below Although there was only a sporadic service of trolleybuses timetabled to turn at Belmont Drive, a fair number of 'extras' worked to this intermediate terminus on the Stormont route. Guy 120 (FZ 7905) is on such a working in December 1962. Belmont Drive was a semi-circular street off Belmont Road with houses around the outer perimeter. The centre of the semi-circle was a grassy area planted with a few trees, and the area is almost unchanged today. A ubiquitous Morris Minor is parked behind the trolleybus. *Richard Whitford*

Above Belfast trolleybuses operated right to Parliament Buildings (unlike the trams, which operated only as far as the back gates of the Stormont estate at Massey Avenue) and used the building as a turning circle. Here 79, identified as an AEC by the unpainted front waist panel, is heading back into the city centre via Albert Bridge on 10 August 1962.

The foundation stone of Parliament Buildings was laid by the Duke of Abercorn in 1928 and the official opening ceremony was performed by the Prince of Wales on 17 November 1932. Many Government Departments operated from Stormont, as the building is popularly referred to after the suburb of Belfast in which it is located. The civil servants, and visitors, supplied significant additional passenger revenue; for example, in 1951 a 10-minute service was provided on each of the Queen's Bridge and Albert Bridge 'legs' of the route, making a 5-minute service between Connswater and Stormont. Although Northern Ireland's system of government changed in 1972, the building still houses civil servants and would be easily capable of refurbishment in the event of a return to a locally based Parliament or Assembly.

The cars parked outside are a very fair representative collection of what top people (and not so top people) were driving in 1962. From left to right are two Morris Minors, a Morris Oxford, an Austin and a Jaguar. On the extreme left is a three-wheel Isetta bubble car made by BMW in their more down-market days! *Denis Battams*

Left Guy BTX 107 (FZ 7892) was photographed by Andrew Bronn in the early 1960s against the backdrop of Parliament Buildings. The trolleybuses did not use the main drive from the Upper Newtownards Road, which was rumoured to be exactly a mile long, but in fact was rather less, but instead sneaked in from the back entrance at Massey Avenue and made their way thence via a side approach. However, once they passed Lord Carson's statue the trolleybuses proudly made their way up the hill to the Main Building. The bus stop was outside the West entrance. *Andrew Bronn*

Above A 'full frontal' view of AEC 98 (FZ 7883) in August 1962, passing through 'Holywood Arches' on its way to the Dundonald terminus outside the Elk Inn. It entered service with Belfast Corporation in 1943 and performed sterling service for 20 years until its retirement in 1963, when all the East Belfast routes were withdrawn and replaced with diesel buses. 'Holywood Arches', or 'The Arches' as it was more commonly known, originally carried the main line of the County Down Railway to Comber, Downpatrick and Newcastle. When that part of the railway was closed by the newly formed Ulster Transport Authority (UTA) in 1950 the overbridge was removed, but the bridge supports remained in situ for many years, creating something of a traffic bottleneck latterly. Adverts for Chivers Jelly and milk adorn the bridge support, while an unofficial, if rather faded, 'GOD IS LOVE' below the 'pinta' advert could do with another coat of paint. *Denis Battams*

Below The bridge supports were subsequently demolished and in February 1996 the whole area is much more 'open'. The main reference points between the two photographs is the three-storey Ulster Bank on the left-hand side of the road and the buildings to the right of it. *Mike Maybin*

Above left There was a turning circle for trolleybuses at the junction of Ormiston Park with Upper Newtownards Road and, like the service to Holywood Arches, that to 'Knock Road' was also a short working of the Dundonald route that operated mainly on Saturday afternoons. Guy 109 (GZ 7894), introduced in 1948, is seen here in September 1962, six years before its retirement. Although its destination suggests that it is about to return to the city centre, the route number should show '18', not '20'. The bus barely visible behind the trolley is one of the new generation of UTA single-deckers introduced initially for tour and private hire work in 1960 and later extended to normal service work.

The garage on the left is still there, although it has changed hands, while on the site of the turning circle itself Texaco opened a filling station about three years ago, although the business had traded from much smaller premises for the previous 14. *Richard Whitford*

Left This view was also taken on the Upper Newtownards Road, although rather nearer the terminus, in which direction the camera is pointed. This time the trolleybus interest is represented by Guy 150 (GZ 8514), which is approaching a stop in the early 1960s. The dark cabinet beside the former tram stop houses the equipment required to feed and isolate sections of the overhead wire in the event of an emergency. All trolleybus systems in the UK (like their tramway predecessors) were required by law to

have section breaks every half mile, and cabinets with the appropriate switchgear were provided along the line of route. For operational convenience these were often combined with 'feeder' points where the power was fed from the generating station to the overhead..

The Knock Evangelical Presbyterian Church, visible between the trolleybus and the stop sign, is still there today. The houses on either side are also unchanged, but the garage further up on the right has become the Stormont Video Shop. *R. F. Mack*

Above On the Upper Newtownards Road in April 1962 Guy BTX 125 (FZ 7910), with GEC electrical equipment and 68-seater Harkness bodywork, waits at the stand for passengers before departing for the city centre. In the background can be seen the outline of the Elk Inn, which marked the terminus of the Dundonald route, and the railings to the right belong to the Dundonald Cemetery, a 42-acre site opened in 1905 which was the eventual terminus of the tramways. Although the trams had been abandoned on the Dundonald route nearly 20 years before this photograph was taken, the pole on which the stop sign is mounted and the box on the nearest traction pole are both relics from that era.

The garage on the right belonging to T. G. Tinsley is currently a Maxol filling station, but the telephone kiosk has disappeared, as have the bus stage sign and trolleybus traction poles. *Colin Routh, courtesy of Andrew Bronn*

Above It is difficult accurately to date this photograph, but from the evidence of the livery, the white-painted bumpers and the absence of direction boards on the signposts, it was probably wartime. The fact that both trolleybuses are operating via Queen's Bridge would suggest that the Albert Bridge 'leg' of the route had not then opened. If that were the case the photograph would have been taken between November 1942 and March 1943.

The vehicle on the left is AEC 76 (FZ 7861), while that on the right is also an AEC, but regretfully cannot be identified. However, one of the characteristics that identified AECs after the war, the unpainted portion of the front waist panel, had not then come into operation.

The rural character of the area is very evident with the turning circle yet to be paved. The 'blind corner' referred to in Hugh McVeigh's memories in the Introduction can clearly be seen to the left of the pub. Then owned by John Bell and advertising 'Old Bushmill's Whiskey' and 'Sandeman's Port', the pub is still very much in business today, albeit under different ownership. *The Deputy Keeper, Public Record Office for Northern Ireland*

Left A contrasting view of Dundonald terminus, taken on 10 August 1962, perhaps 20 years after the one above. Guy 118 (FZ 7903) is just about to start its return journey to the city. The pub has not greatly changed in the intervening period, although the centre entrance in the previous photograph has been replaced by a side door. The new owners have retained the Old Bushmills sign, but that for Sandeman's has disappeared. The aptness of the new owners' surname for the Elk Inn is more than a happy coincidence, I should think! *Denis Battams*

Above Guy BTX 106 (FZ 7891) is in East Bridge Street returning to the City Hall in about 1962; the camera is pointing out of town. This is one of the relatively rare occasions when the destination is incorrectly displayed. The advertisement for Jacob's Cream Crackers on the upper panels would be just as relevant today.

The motor bus going in the opposite direction is one of the hundred bought from London Transport in 1953 to speed up the tram replacement programme. Although seven or eight years old when purchased by Belfast, they were rebodied by Harkness Coachworks and the majority lasted in service until the 1970s. Regrettably many were destroyed in the civil disturbances of that time. The other trolleybus is too far away to be identified. The old-style tram stop attached to the third traction pole on the right was replaced with the Edinburgh-style stops in the mid-1960s.

The large building on the left is the Corporation Electricity Department's generating station. This was opened in 1898 and extended in 1905 to provide power for the newly-electrified tramway system. It was demolished about 1980 and the site is derelict at present. All the buildings in the right background comprising Short Strand and Albertbridge Road have also been demolished and replaced by modern low-rise dwellings. Visible in the picture are a Hillman Minx and a Ford Consul. *R. F. Mack*

Right AEC 96 (FZ 7881), returning to the City Hall from Dundonald, is captured on 15 September 1962 while passing the junction of Woodstock Road and Albertbridge Road. Shortly after Short Strand Depot was opened the area was made into a traffic roundabout and over-head 'sidings' were installed for Albertbridge Road buses (ie Dundonald and Stormont) and Woodstock Road buses (ie Bloomfield and Cregagh).

The car about to head up Woodstock Road is a Ford Prefect. Note the inverted 'U'-shaped hoods above the pedestrian crossings, a short-lived experiment to focus the lighting on to the crossings. This area has since been completely redeveloped into a major traffic junction, and none of the houses and small shops in this photograph have survived. *Richard Whitford*

Above The day before the Castlereagh route was closed for trolleybus operation, 19 January 1963, 64 (FZ 7849) was photographed in Castlereagh Street, crossing Albertbridge Road; the view is looking towards the city centre. It was one of the first 'production' batch of AECs placed in service by the Corporation in 1940-43; this particular vehicle was introduced in 1942 and retired in 1963, having given 21 years of (almost) trouble-free service. The unpainted front nearside panel can clearly be seen, while the advertisement for 'Old Friends Guinness' reminds us of one of Ireland's most enduring products.

The overhead wiring was quite complex here. The normal services through the junction were to Stormont/Dundonald via Albert Bridge, which operated along Albertbridge Road, and to Castlereagh, which operated from Mountpottinger Road into Castlereagh Street (and vice versa). However, the wiring was arranged in such a way as to allow trolleybuses to and from Castlereagh to operate also along Albertbridge Road to gain access to Haymarket Depot. As well as this, there was a 'slip' wire from Mountpottinger Road into Albertbridge Road in the out-of-town direction; this was a carry-over from tram days, and was not used by trolleybuses on a regular basis.

Most of the buildings on the left-hand side of Albertbridge Road have been demolished, while those on the right have been replaced by red-brick one- and two-storey houses. The road itself is a dual carriageway. *Richard Whitford*

Left AEC 49 (FZ 7834), fitted with GEC electrical equipment and Harkness 68-seater bodywork, runs along Beersbridge Road on 3 November 1962. It is heading towards the city centre, and it is not clear if the young man is hoping to board the bus or just interested. In many ways this photograph typifies a perception of working-class Belfast, with the two-storey terrace houses and corner shops. However, without at all wishing to appear snobbish, the (rather old) Riley car is not typical of what one might expect from such an area over 30 years ago. The Morris Minor on the left was one of the most popular small family cars of the period and sold well over one million in the UK.

Tamery Street, which is marked by the large advertisement, and all the houses visible in the photograph have since been demolished and replaced by a modern low-rise red-brick estate. The area is totally unrecognisable today. *Richard Whitford*

Guy 121 (FZ 7906) emerges from Castlereagh Street and crosses Beersbridge Road into Castlereagh Road en route (not surprisingly!) to Castlereagh. Although undated, I would estimate that the photograph was taken about 1961 or 1962. The camera is looking towards the city centre.

The overhead wiring was relatively simple at this junction. The two routes that passed through were to Castlereagh, as already mentioned, and to Bloomfield, which operated along Beersbridge Road. It is believed that a slip wire to allow trolleybuses to work from Castlereagh Street into Beersbridge Road was provided until about 1948.

In some ways the changes to this junction have not been as dramatic as with some others in East Belfast. The street layout can still be clearly recognised and the majority of the buildings are still in place. Perhaps the main difference is that the small triangular site of houses and pubs just visible behind the trolleybus have been demolished to give much better sight lines. *Robert Mack/Mike Maybin*

Above left Guy BTX 120 (FZ 7905), with GEC electrical equipment and Harkness 68-seater bodywork, passes the Vono bedding depot in Beersbridge Road en route to Bloomfield in the early 1960s. The trolleybus overhead has been constructed using the 'gantry' method, which joined opposite tramway poles with steel tubes to give added strength to support the much heavier trolleybus overhead equipment.

The former Vono factory is now Owen O'Cork mills, while the building next door, which used to be the Elmwood Carpet Cleaning Company, is now Discount Windows. Steen's Row of single-storey whitewashed cottages has been demolished, and the area is now wasteground. The telephone vans are both Morrises, the nearer one a Mini and the other a Minor. *Robert Mack*

Left Snow is not a frequent visitor to Belfast, particularly not snow like this! I well remember that winter of 1963 when our school was closed for a week and I took the opportunity to go to Belfast (we lived in Bangor) to see how the trolleybuses were coping. There were several routes where the hills were too steep to allow the wheels to get a proper grip on the packed snow, and where the service had to be cut back for a few days; the Upper Oldpark Road to Carr's Glen and the drive from Stormont gates to Parliament Buildings were two examples. Most firms allowed their employees to leave early as public transport was severely disrupted, although trolleybuses did operate on most routes, albeit with difficulty, as this view of Guy 197 (GZ 8561) at Bloomfield terminus shows. The passengers look most uncomfortable, and one can imagine their relief at getting into the warm bus.

The new Edinburgh-style bus stops had not been fully introduced at this stage (no pun intended!), and the periscope-shaped contraption next to it is a time clock. These were introduced to try to 'encourage' crews to keep better time, specifically by not leav-

ing the terminus early, but they lasted only a few years. Within a short time conductors discovered that by quickly moving the handle that operated the time stamp on the waybill it had the effect of moving the time on a few minutes. Many conductors would therefore insert a piece of scrap paper, rattle the handle several times, then insert the waybill. The few minutes gained were made up at the next timing point.

The only change to this scene today is the absence of the telephone kiosk and the time clock. A new bus shelter has been supplied and is a welcome addition, now that the waiting period between buses can be 15 minutes. When this photograph was taken, the off-peak frequency was 8 minutes, increasing to a bus every 2½ minutes at busy times! Just behind the time clock a Morris Minor is lurking, and it rather looks as if it has been fitted with chains for the occasion. *The Deputy Keeper, Public Record Office for Northern Ireland*

Above Guy 175 (GZ 8539) is parked at Bloomfield terminus in the early 1960s. The rhetorical 'Had your daily pinta yet?' was a popular advertising campaign aimed at getting people to drink more milk, not beer! Bloomfield was the last of the East Belfast tram routes to be converted to trolleybuses, and although wired for trolleys during the war, the rubber-tyred vehicles did not appear until 1946. The old-style 'Keep Left' traffic sign can be seen to the left of the picture, while the conductor is carefully looking from behind the trolleybus as if about to cross a very busy road! An Austin A40, Ford Anglia and the almost inevitable Morris Minor can all be seen in the photograph.

The shops are still there today, exactly the same apart from several changes of ownership, and the only other difference is that the 'Keep Left' signs have been replaced with modern ones. *Colin Routh, courtesy of Andrew Bronn*

Left The quality of this photograph is relatively poor but I have included it since very few were taken of the ex-Wolverhampton trolleybuses in service. This is 242 (DDA 992, fleet number 292 in Wolverhampton) in Albertbridge Road in the early 1950s. The four-wheel chassis and the curvature of the rear offside window in the lower saloon are the main identifying features of its Wolverhampton origins. It is on the Oval Grounds service, which was mainly used for football specials, this being the nearest turning point to the Glentoran FC ground.

The bus visible behind is R276 (originally R812, FZ 233), an AEC Regent. It was bought new in 1938 by the Northern Ireland Road Transport Board (NIRTB), the precursor to the Ulster Transport Authority (UTA), which itself preceded the present operator Ulsterbus and was the main operator of the country routes. This location, near the junction with Mountpottinger Road, has been completely revamped to make way for a new traffic scheme. *Photographer unknown, courtesy of David Harvey*

Below Albertbridge Road in the early 1960s, and Guy 165 (GZ 8529) is en route to Dundonald. The intersecting street ahead of the trolleybus is Templemore Avenue, with its old-style 'Keep Left' signs; even by the date of this photograph these signs were still gas-lit. The Mountpottinger YMCA (on the left) is still in business, although without its neon sign. The corner shop is owned by Magee's and has been tastefully decorated. Mountpottinger Orange Hall with its Union flag is the tall building on the right, while between it and the entrance to Templemore Avenue, Nabney's china shop has since been converted to Keen Suites on the left and the Vinyl Centre at the corner. The gasometer faintly visible in the distance was demolished recently. *Robert Mack*

Above No 99 (FZ 7884) is heading down Castlereagh Road in the direction of Castle Junction. The advertisement along the upper side panel (known as the 'decency' panel in horse tram days) is for Bass beer, still a local favourite! The traction poles were formerly used to support the tram overhead and can be identified by the spiked finial on the top. The street lights were also mounted on the tram poles, with an extension piece in place of the finial.

The houses on the left have been replaced by a Stewart's/Crazy Prices supermarket, while the garage on the same side is now a Shell filling station. The cars on the left are a Ford Prefect and a Ford Popular, and the tanker on the right is a Comet belonging to Cregagh Dairies. *Richard Whitford*

Right I have often wondered why there was a reversing triangle at Houston Park on the Castlereagh Road, given that the terminus was only a very short distance further up the road. Part of the reasoning may lie in the fact that the tram terminus

was at this point and that, in general, trolleybus turning facilities initially reflected the location of tram termini and crossovers. Nevertheless there were regular early morning journeys timetabled to Houston Park, which used route number 32 from 1951 until the end of trolleybus operation on the route; this number was later reallocated to the bus route 'Braniel via Castlereagh'.

In this view, taken by Richard Whitford in November 1962, BUT 187 (GZ 8551) has just reversed from Castlereagh Road into Houston Park and is about to turn right to return towards the city centre, although the destination screen suggests that 187 is about to return to Haymarket Depot; if so, it will follow the Castlereagh route into town as far as Mountpottinger Junction, where it will turn left into Albertbridge Road, cross the Albert Bridge and enter the depot via Stewart Street. There has been no change to the buildings in the photograph, and the car turning left into Houston Park is a Singer. *Richard Whitford*

Above A nice three-quarter view of AEC 91 (FZ 7876) taken in the early 1960s on Castlereagh Road. The street on the right, from which the car is emerging, is Houston Park, seen in the previous photograph; as the frogs were sprung, the conductor did not need to operate them and his main job was to help the driver to reverse safely. The old-style 'Bus Stop' sign is mounted on the specially painted traction pole, but the tramway 'section box' below is actually for the overhead street lighting, the power for which was carried on separate overhead wires mounted several feet above the trolleybus ones. The location of the city boundary is clearly marked, not only with the official sign on the left of the picture, but also with the difference in road surfacing! *Robert Mack*

Below Another view of Castlereagh Road taken nearer the terminus showing Guy 108 (FZ 7893) and BUT 206 (GZ 8570). After the war the Northern Ireland Government embarked on a series of job promotion measures aimed at retaining the high employment level generated by the hostilities. As part of this they created a number of industrial estates, one of which was at Castlereagh Road. Many factories were built including Lord Roberts Memorial Workshop seen on the left of this photograph; regretfully it is not in use at present. The next door factory, with the three square windows, was Hughes tool factory, now Hughes Christiensen.

It was hoped that these measures would generate significant additional traffic for the trolleybuses and a siding was laid in from the workshops long enough to accommodate a large number of vehicles; the start of the siding can just be seen to the left of the trolleybus. However, a combination of an increase in the use of private cars and a relocation of many of the workers from inner-city Belfast to 'leafy suburbs' like Ballygowan, Saintfield and Bangor rendered the siding redundant soon after it was built. The broken-down fence on the right has since been replaced by a more modern structure, while the telegraph wires have been relocated underground, rendering the pole unnecessary! *Robert Mack*

Right It is not possible accurately to date this photograph, but it is either the late 1940s or, more likely, early 1950s, judging by the livery, the 'BELFAST CORPORATION' title along the waist band of the trolleybus and the rural character of the area. AECs 32 (FZ 7817) and 29 (FZ 7814) are at Castlereagh at the 'end of the lines', as the terminus was often called in Belfast - a hangover from tramcar days. At the time of this photograph there was a reverser at the terminus; to turn, trolleybuses crossed Knockbreda Road into Ballygowan Road (or Hillfoot Road as it was then known), then reversed left into Knockbreda Road. They then turned right into Castlereagh Road and parked at the stop. The crews' rest room facilities were provided 'naturally', as seen in the photograph.

The triangle above the number plate on 32 was a combination stop light and direction indicator box. These were soon replaced by the standard flashing amber lights for direction and twin red lights for braking. The photograph was taken looking away from the city centre. *R. C. Jackson*

Below This view was taken at the same place perhaps ten years later, showing how the area had developed in that relatively short period. The reverser at the terminus has been replaced by a turning circle, built just about where the crew in the previous photograph had been enjoying a well-earned rest.

Castlereagh was one of the busiest routes in the 1950s and '60s and no fewer than four trolleybuses are seen here, those whose numbers are visible being AEC 102 (FZ 7887) and Guy 121 (FZ 7906). The 'STAGE' stop on the right is an old tram stop, although the tram terminus was at the city boundary near Houston Park. The housing estate to the right was public authority stock built by the Northern Ireland Housing Trust. *R. C. Jackson*

Top This photograph of Guy 168 (GZ 8532) was taken somewhere on the Cregagh route in the early 1960s. I have had some difficulty in identifying the location and of course the background buildings may have been demolished a number of years ago; if any reader can help I would be glad to hear from them via the publisher. No 168 was donated in 1968 to the National Trolleybus Association for preservation. *Robert Mack*

Middle Guy 152 (GZ 8516) at Bell's Bridge roundabout on the Cregagh Road some time in the early 1960s. The upper panel advertisement for 'Rentaset' reflected the early days of television when many people preferred to rent rather than buy one. Although it is hard to imagine in these days of reliable televisions, many people experienced real anxiety about cathode ray tubes breaking down. A new tube cost about £60 - about three weeks' wages at that time.

When the Cregagh Road route opened for trolleybus operation in 1941 a reverser was built at Graham Gardens; trolleybuses reversed left into that street, which was the one below Ladas Drive seen here to the right. With the development of Mount Merrion Avenue and the construction of the roundabout the reverser was replaced by a turning circle.

The frog here was electrically operated. Most intermediate turning circles had hand-operated frogs, but the danger for the conductor in crossing the road at this point, combined with the disruption to traffic caused by the trolleybus stopping in the middle of the roundabout, persuaded the Corporation to install an electrically operated automatic frog. The 'skate' can just be seen on the right-hand wire.

By the time of this photograph, curved segments had been developed for trolleybus overhead, which allowed tight curves to present a much smoother path to the trolley heads than a large number of 'pull-offs'. Therefore higher speeds could be attained with less risk of de-wirement. These segments can be seen on the roundabout curve.

There has been no change to the buildings in the photograph. The only discernible difference between the 1960s and now is that the kerbstones on the roundabout are no longer painted black and white.

The vehicles in the photograph are the rear end of a Morris van parked outside the newsagents shop, a BMC 7-ton lorry and a Mini van. *Robert Mack*

Bottom This view of Cregagh terminus, looking away from the city centre, was taken in the early 1950s and shows Guy 169 (GZ 8533) about to begin the cross-town journey to Carr's Glen. The bus carries the familiar 'Don't be vague, Ask for Haig' whisky advert.

The street to the left is Cregagh Park, while the road across the top is Upper Knockbreda Road. This area has changed considerably since this photograph was taken. Both Cregagh Road and Knockbreda Road have been greatly widened, and the view is now of a large road junction. The houses to the left are, however, very much the same, although they have lost some garden as a result of the road widening schemes. New houses have been built approximately where the trees are in the centre of the picture. The turning circle is still used by Citybus, although two buses out of three now turn right along the Knockbreda dual carriageway to the Ormeau turning circle at Forster Green Hospital. *R. C. Jackson*

BELFAST TROLLEYBUSES 1938-1968

Another view of the turning circle, looking in the opposite direction, about ten years later. AEC 26 (FZ 7811) was one of the first of the 'production' trolleybuses to be introduced to Belfast in 1941 to work the East Belfast services. Coincidentally Cregagh was the first of these routes to be converted that year, so it is possible that 26 had been working the Cregagh route for the previous 21 years before this photograph was taken in 1962. It is about to operate the cross-town service to Carr's Glen, while behind it AEC 58 (FZ 7844) is on the Cregagh to City Hall route. (Because the

frequency of service to Cregagh was twice that to Carr's Glen, every second vehicle turned at the City Hall.)

The red brick building behind 58 belonged to Castlereagh District Council; it is now fulfilling an identical function for Castlereagh Borough Council, and has recently acquired an extension. The turning circle is virtually unchanged today - right down to the hard-wearing square sets! The houses across the Cregagh Road are also unchanged. *Denis Battams*

SOUTH BELFAST

THIS AREA comprises the section of the city from Cregagh Road to the Donegall Road, and the only tramcar route in the area converted to trolleybuses was Ormeau Road in 1948. However, there were ambitious plans to operate trolleybuses on the Stranmillis Road, Malone Road, Lisburn Road and Donegall Road, but with the change of General Manager in 1951 from Robert McCreary to Joseph Mackle, this policy was reversed and a large number of Daimler motor buses were bought with the express purpose of converting the remaining tram routes as quickly as possible.

I have often wondered what the trolleybus overhead layout would have been like at Shaftesbury Square in the 1950s, when no fewer than 11 routes would have operated through it. I suspect that it would have been the most impressive junction on the system!

The Ormeau Road route was provided with a turning circle at Rosetta, and although in later years trolleybuses were not shown in the timetable as turning there, there was an irregular use of the facility. Unlike most intermediate turning circles, Rosetta was equipped with an automatic frog, which can easily be seen on the outer wire just above the vehicle. This was installed on the same grounds of road safety that applied at Bell's Bridge. AEC 82 (FZ 7867) is on its way south to Ormeau Road terminus in the mid-1950s, and old-style gas-lit 'Keep Left' signs are installed on the roundabout. The Roman Catholic Convent of Nazareth House, which cared for children and elderly people, showed an impressive view to the Ormeau Road. The view today is virtually identical save that the traffic signs on the roundabout have been replaced with those of the current design. *William Montgomery*

Right Trolleybus routes in South Belfast.

BELFAST TROLLEYBUSES 1938-1968

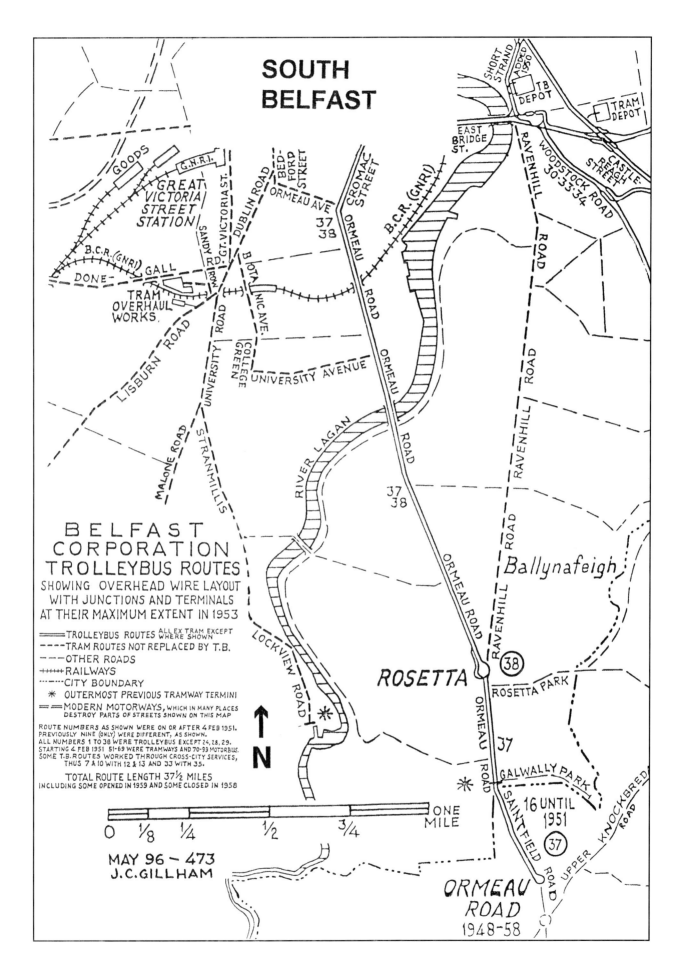

SOUTH BELFAST

GOODS

G.N.R.I.

GREAT
VICTORIA
STREET
STATION

SHORT
STRAND

ADDED
1950

TB
DEPOT

TRAM
DEPOT

CASTLE-
REAGH
STREET

EAST
BRIDGE
ST.

WOODSTOCK ROAD
30.33.34

B.C.R.(GNRI)

DUBLIN ROAD

BEDFORD STREET

ORMEAU AVE.
37
38

CROMAC STREET

B.C.R.(GNRI)

SANDY ROW

GT.VICTORIA ST.

GALL

DONE-

TRAM
OVERHAUL
WORKS.

BOTANIC AVE.

UNIVERSITY ROAD

COLLEGE GREEN

UNIVERSITY AVENUE

LISBURN ROAD

MALONE ROAD

STRANMILLIS

RIVER LAGAN

ORMEAU ROAD

RAVENHILL ROAD

RAVENHILL ROAD

Ballynafeigh

37
38

ORMEAU ROAD

BELFAST
CORPORATION
TROLLEYBUS ROUTES
SHOWING OVERHEAD WIRE LAYOUT
WITH JUNCTIONS AND TERMINALS
AT THEIR MAXIMUM EXTENT IN 1953

══════ TROLLEYBUS ROUTES ALL EX TRAM EXCEPT WHERE SHOWN
------ TRAM ROUTES NOT REPLACED BY T.B.
— — OTHER ROADS
+++++ RAILWAYS
·—·—· CITY BOUNDARY
✳ OUTERMOST PREVIOUS TRAMWAY TERMINI
══ MODERN MOTORWAYS, WHICH IN MANY PLACES
   DESTROY PARTS OF STREETS SHOWN ON THIS MAP

ROUTE NUMBERS AS SHOWN WERE ON OR AFTER 4 FEB 1951.
PREVIOUSLY NINE (ONLY) WERE DIFFERENT, AS SHOWN.
ALL NUMBERS 1 TO 38 WERE TROLLEYBUS EXCEPT 24,28,29.
STARTING 4 FEB 1951 51-69 WERE TRAMWAYS AND 70-99 MOTORBUS.
SOME T.B.ROUTES WORKED THROUGH CROSS-CITY SERVICES,
   THUS 7 & 10 WITH 12 & 13 AND 33 WITH 35.

TOTAL ROUTE LENGTH 37½ MILES
INCLUDING SOME OPENED IN 1959 AND SOME CLOSED IN 1958

↑
N

LOCKVIEW ROAD

ROSETTA

38

RAVENHILL ROAD

ROSETTA PARK

37

GALWALLY PARK

16 UNTIL
1951

37

SAINTFIELD ROAD

UPPER KNOCKBRED ROAD

| 0 | ⅛ | ¼ | ½ | ¾ | ONE MILE |

MAY 96 ~ 473
J.C.GILLHAM

ORMEAU
ROAD
1948-58

Trolleybuses were introduced on the Ormeau Road route in 1948 and were replaced by diesel buses in 1958, so there was much less opportunity to photograph them there than in many other places. This view of BUT 206 (GZ 8570) was taken in the early 1950s near the terminus, and we are looking towards the city centre; the car heading down Saintfield Road is an Austin 10.

The rural character of the area has been completely changed and it is now a major traffic intersection. The second photograph was taken in February 1996 and about the only reference point with the earlier view is the hedge on the left-hand side of the road. The entire right-hand side of Saintfield Road has been given over to commercial premises, the largest of which is the Supermac shopping complex, one of the first of Northern Ireland's out-of-town superstores. *R. C. Jackson/Mike Maybin*

This view of AEC 77 (FZ 7862) was also taken by Ralph Jackson, and dates from the early 1950s judging by the 'BELFAST CORPORATION' legend on the waist panels of both buses. From 1948 to 1958 both buses and trolleybuses shared a common terminus at 'Fortbreda', as the Ormeau Road terminus was called officially in the timetables. The trolleybuses operated from Victoria Square in the city centre via Cromac Street to Ormeau terminus and carried the route number 37 in both directions. Motor buses to Ormeau used the 'inside track' at the terminus as they required a slightly smaller turning circle. The houses across the road were later demolished to make way for a road link near Upper Galwally, and this view is unrecognisable today. *R. C. Jackson*

THE FOLLOWING selection of photographs were all taken between 1963 and the closure of the system in 1968, and I have chosen them to illustrate the main classes of trolleybuses operated in Belfast - the AECs, Guys, BUTs (both types) and the Sunbeam. Equally I have tried to cover the main areas of the city where the trolleybus was the primary form of public transport for many years. With one exception all are from the collection of Richard Whitford.

Top Richard Whitford photographed Guy 19 (FZ 7894) on 10 August 1963 en route to Cregagh a few weeks before the route was converted to motor buses. No 109 is beautifully turned out and was not withdrawn until 1968, having completed 20 years in service. The buildings behind the trolleybus were demolished to make way for RAC House, completed about 1980. The attractive three-storey red-brick building on the far side of Chichester Street was Her Majesty's Stationary Office, replaced by IDB House about 1960. *Richard Whitford*

Middle This area is entirely changed from when the photograph was taken on 3 August 1963. The trolleybus is in Albertbridge Road; the road to the left leads to the Albert Bridge and thence to the city centre, while the street to the right is Woodstock Street.

Short Strand bus depot was behind the houses, while the waste ground to the left was used as a traffic roundabout. Trolleybuses were provided with two sets of overhead wires, the inner of which went to Woodstock Road and was used by Cregagh and Bloomfield routes, while the outer pair was used by Stormont and Dundonald vehicles. AEC 96 (FZ 7891) is heading for Cregagh on the cross-town route from Carr's Glen, and sadly appears to be rather in need of a repaint. *Richard Whitford*

Bottom BUT 224 (OZ 7326) passes McKee & Greer's Drapers Agents on the same day. Both the shop and the little 'kitchen' houses to the left have been swept away and the road is now a cul-de-sac known as Woodstock Place. Through traffic uses a new road, Woodstock Link. An Inglis bread van and a Morris Minor van are visible in the background. *Richard Whitford*

Top Perhaps the most photogenic route operated by Belfast trolleybuses was that to Parliament Buildings in East Belfast. When the Northern Ireland Parliament was established in 1921 it met initially in the Belfast City Hall, then moved to Assembly's College, Belfast, until the official opening of the Parliament Buildings at Stormont in 1932.

When trolleybuses replaced trams on the Stormont route, the Government asked the Corporation to extend the service to Parliament Buildings itself, and overhead wires were erected from the tram terminus at the Massey Avenue gates, past Lord Carson's statue and round the back of the Parliament Building. This view of Guy 124 (FZ 7909) was taken at the Massey Avenue entrance in the early 1960s. The advertisement for Nelson cigarettes at 3/10d (about 19p) for 20 reminds us of the inflation of the late 1960s and early '70s. *British Trolleybus Society*

Middle I presume that the traffic lights are at red for the trolleybus, as the two ladies are otherwise taking something of a chance in alighting from BUT 221 here in York Street, even if 12 May 1968 (the date of the photograph) was a Sunday! The building to the left is still there, although derelict and up for sale. The Fashion Supermarket, formerly Henry's stores, has been demolished and is currently an empty space. The main Co-Operative building is still there, although now physically connected to the University of Ulster on the other side of the road by a covered pedestrian walkway at second-storey level. *Richard Whitford*

Bottom Sunbeam 246 (2206 OI) was intended to be the forerunner of a fleet of 100 new trolleybuses, but for a variety of reasons, including the decision of London Transport to abandon trolleybus operation, this was not to be and instead the Corporation chose to purchase motor buses. The trolleybus, on a tour sponsored by the National Trolleybus Association, has just been repainted and is in 'ex-works' condition, preparatory to being handed over to the London Trolleybus Preservation Society for preservation. The rear dome was painted khaki to minimise the effects of the graphite, which was used to lubricate the wires, falling on the roof.

The photograph was taken on 15 April 1968 on Shore Road on the city side of Faith Tabernacle. The wall advertisement for 'Ormo' bread is still relevant, although the company has since changed its logo. This area has undergone very little change since the photograph was taken. *Richard Whitford*

THE FIRST route to be converted from tramcars to trolley-buses was Falls Road on 28 March 1938. Initially the service operated only to Fruithill Park on the Andersonstown Road, but it was extended to a turning circle at Casement Park in 1954. In 1952 a short branch was built from Falls Park along the Glen Road to a terminus at Binigan Drive near St Theresa's Church.

In 1959 a further branch was opened from City Cemetery to a turning circle at Divismore Crescent in Ballymurphy by way of Whiterock Road and Springfield Road.

There were plans to operate trolleybuses along the Springfield Road to Ballymurphy and via West Circular Road, Ballygomartin Road and Twaddell Avenue to Ardoyne, but these were abandoned with Joseph Mackle's appointment to the General Managership in 1951.

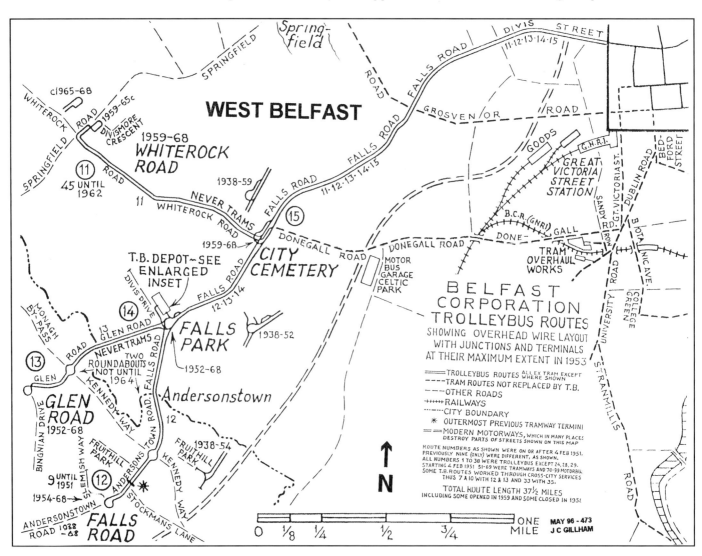

Trolleybus routes in West Belfast.

Right This view was taken on the Falls Road in the mid-1960s within a few years of the trolleybuses being replaced by diesels, and shows 202 (GZ 8566), a BUT with GEC electrical equipment and locally built Harkness 68-seater bodywork, en route to Glen Road. The destination display suggests that it was on a cross-city run from Whitewell in North Belfast. The new Edinburgh-style bus stop signs have been erected and one is seen here attached to the near traction pole. The area is almost unchanged today. *Robert Mack*

Below Suburban West Belfast in the peaceful 1950s. No 130 (GZ 1621) was about to return to Haymarket Depot when photographed by an unknown enthusiast (the camera is pointing in the direction of the terminus). No 130 was one of the two wartime Sunbeams delivered in 1943 to a very utilitarian design, was refurbished shortly after the war to a less harsh specification. It was fitted with British Thompson-Houston electrical equipment and Park Royal 56-seater bodywork. Like the semi-utility Sunbeams, which entered service in 1946, it had only four wheels.

The advertisement for Andrews powders was a popular one to grace the sides of Belfast trolleybuses at that time and could certainly be bought in Charles Quinn's chemist shop at the corner of Rockville Street. The shop is still there today, although trading as McKenzie's Pharmacy. The row of three-storey houses behind the trolleybus is also still intact. *Photographer unknown*

Right On the last day of trolleybus operation, 12 May 1968, this unusual view of Guy 112 (FZ 7897) was taken at the junction of Falls Road and Glen Road during a farewell tour organised by the National Trolleybus Association (NTA). In order to cover as much of the overhead wiring as possible in the time available, the Association hired 112 and worked out an itinerary, one part of which was to drive from Falls Road terminus to Falls Park and turn left up Glen Road to the terminus there. However, the overhead wiring did not allow this to be done directly, so the driver had to position his vehicle carefully under the junction of the wires and remove his trolleys from the Falls Road wires and transfer them to the Glen Road pair.

No 112 was scheduled for preservation by the NTA and prepared for the handover by the Belfast Corporation to 'ex-works' standard, as this photograph shows clearly. The few spectators to the right of the picture are all enthusiasts on the tour, while the cemetery behind the trolleybus is Milltown, the main Roman Catholic burying place for the City of Belfast. The scene is virtually unchanged today. *R. F. Payne*

Below Thirty years earlier this posed view was taken prior to the official opening in March 1938. Crossley 3 (EZ 7891), with Metro-Vick electrical equipment and Crossley bodywork, was photographed outside Falls Depot on 11 January of that year. The curved windows upstairs at the front and rear are one of the Crossley trademarks. Although Belfast owned only two

Crossleys, Manchester and other operators in the North West bought large numbers and the distinctive appearance of the upstairs windows was a common sight in that part of the country for many years.

The relatively well-dressed spectators suggest that this was an 'occasion' of some importance. The scaffolding in the background was being used to put the finishing touches to the overhead wiring, and the little pile of rubble to the left marks the spot where the roundabout will eventually be built. The horse trough on the left was later replaced by a more modern structure and relocated nearer the roadside. The car outside Magee's chemist shop is a Morris 8. *William Montgomery*

Above Guy 106 (FZ 7891) was photographed in Andersonstown Road on 21 January 1964 when the area was being cleared for the construction of Kennedy Way, a new road built to link the Stockman's Lane exit of the M1 with Monagh Road and Turf Lodge via Andersonstown Road and Glen Road, at the junctions with which roundabouts were constructed. This photograph shows work in progress; the new trolleybus overhead wires to be used on the roundabout when it is constructed can be seen to the right of 106, 'tied off' to a traction pole.

The advertisement on the side of the bus is for Jacob's biscuits - a brand probably even more popular now than when this photograph was taken over 30 years ago. The houses opposite are still there and relatively little changed. *Richard Whitford*

Below Guy 119 (FZ 7904) is seen at the same location, but with the camera pointing towards the terminus. The date is 12 September 1964 and the roundabout has now been built; the new portion of garden wall can clearly be seen in both pictures, and the new road surface is clearly visible. Protective pedestrian barriers have also been installed and the new overhead wiring is in use. *Richard Whitford*

Above BUT 199 (GZ 8563) was photographed by Ed Humphreys on the Falls Road on 29 March 1967 en route to Casement Park. The overhead wiring is supported by the tubular form of construction that enabled old tram standards to be re-used. The MS garage and the white single-storey building on the left are no longer in existence; the latter was demolished to make way for the Westway Bingo Club. The red-brick wall on the right has given way to a modern fence of iron railings, behind which a new shopping centre has been built. *E. M. H. Humphreys*

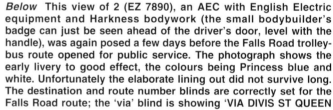

Below This view of 2 (EZ 7890), an AEC with English Electric equipment and Harkness bodywork (the small bodybuilder's badge can just be seen ahead of the driver's door, level with the handle), was again posed a few days before the Falls Road trolleybus route opened for public service. The photograph shows the early livery to good effect, the colours being Princess blue and white. Unfortunately the elaborate lining out did not survive long. The destination and route number blinds are correctly set for the Falls Road route; the 'via' blind is showing 'VIA DIVIS ST QUEEN ST WELLINGTON PL & DONEGALL PL', and 'VIA GROSVENOR RD' is peeking out below. Regretfully, in spite of plans to do so, trolleybuses never made it to Grosvenor Road. The off-side trafficator is located beside the side light and was replaced in later years by amber flashing lights.

Telegraph poles with multiple insulators, like the one visible in the distance, were a common sight in suburban Belfast between the wars. The area immediately around Fruithill Park is little changed today. *William Montgomery*

Right Fleet number 1 (EZ 7889), an AEC with English Electric equipment and 68-seater Harkness bodywork, was still carrying trade plates when photographed early in 1938. Before the trolleybus service proper started, driver training was carried out on the upper part of the route and it is probable that this photograph was taken then.

The trolleybus is in the early livery of white front and blue lower side panels, and carries the destination 'CASTLE JUNCTION' (appropriate for the Falls Road route) with the 'via' blind showing 'VIA HIGH ST QUEEN'S BDG & MOUNTPOTTINGER RD' (appropriate for the Castlereagh route). The route number is set at '38', appropriate for the Ormeau Road route - which was not to be trolleybus operated for another ten years!

The location is Fruithill Park. From 1938 until June 1954 this was the trolleybus terminus, and there was a reverser. In 1954 the route was extended to Casement Park, a few hundred yards further up Andersonstown Road. The scene today is almost identical to when this photograph was taken nearly 60 years ago, although the telegraph pole is now on the left-hand side of the street, the telephone kiosk is no longer there and the wall to the right has been replaced by a wooden fence. *A. Ratcliffe*

Below After having studied the performance of the various chassis, bodies and makes of electrical equipment in various combinations within the batch of experimental vehicles, the Corporation standardised on AECs with GEC electrical equipment and Harkness 68-seater bodywork, and 16 (FZ 7801) was one of the first of the standard batch. Initially the Corporation had ordered 114, but government control of wartime production resulted in the order summarily being reduced to 88. However, as most other cities had to do with much less, Belfast did not protest.

No 16 is located at the Fruithill Park terminus, but the destination displays are all (correctly) set for Cregagh, which opened for trolleybuses in February 1941. The wartime livery was then in force, which reduced the overall 'white' look of the front to a more sombre white above and blue below. The lining out has all but disappeared.

The white line on the road is to help drivers judge where to stop before carrying out the reversing manoeuvre into Fruithill Park. Similarly the black and white painted kerbstones in the background were felt to be helpful in blackout conditions. The only changes at this location today are that the kerbstones are no longer painted and the waist-high wall to the left of the picture is now about 10 feet tall. *Deputy Keeper, Public Record Office for Northern Ireland*

BUT 197 (GZ 8557) was captured outside Casement Park on 23 March 1967, just over a year before Falls Road was to lose its trolleybuses permanently. The turning circle was one of the tightest in Belfast and without the curved 'segment'-style overhead there would have been a need for lots more traction poles, not to mention a veritable 'cat's cradle' of supportive span wires. The container at the base of the traction pole was for sand. The advertisement on the side of the bus modestly extols the London Mantle Warehouse, then trading at Castle Street, Chapel Lane and North Street, as offering 'Belfast's most wanted fashions'! The more prosaic 'Red Heart' bottled Guinness is said to be 'so consistently good'.

Note the old-style 'school' sign to the left of the main traction pole. The turning circle was returned to the Gaelic Athletic Association (GAA) authorities a number of years ago and has been incorporated into the Park. *E. M. H. Humphreys*

Above In 1957 Glen Road terminus was out in the country with the Black Mountain clearly visible in the background. On 9 September 1957 AEC 33 (FZ 7818) prepares to leave on a cross-town journey to Whitehouse. The lower destination display reads 'VIA QUEENS BRIDGE YORK ST & PASSES N COUNTIES RLY'. This is quite wrong and should read 'VIA QUEEN ST . . .' However, I doubt if many Belfast people were seriously incommoded by the error - it was repeated on quite a few 'via' trolleybus blinds of that time.

The 'Model Orange' bottled by McKenna & McGinley and reputedly enjoyed by a well-known reverend gentleman, might be held to be an unusual advertisement in such a 'green' area! *Denis Battams*

Below This view of BUT 195 (GZ 8559) was taken at exactly the same place on 12 August 1962. The new St Theresa's school has been built in the meantime and greatly obscures the view of Black Mountain. Out of sight of the picture and to the right of the school there was a complex of Roman Catholic church, convent, presbytery and training school for young offenders. With the exception of the latter, known as St Patrick's, the other establishments all took the name St Theresa's after the church, and in time the area acquired the name too. Current Citybus timetables refer to the terminus as 'St Theresa's, Glen Road'. *Denis Battams*

Above The climb from Falls Road to Whiterock Road turning circle on the Springfield Road was one of the steepest in the city, but the trolleybuses had no trouble even when fully laden. This early 1960s view shows Guy 172 (GZ 8536) en route to Whiterock terminus before the route number changed from 45 to 11. The Gresham paint and wallpaper shop advertised on the upper side panel regretfully no longer trades from the street from which it derived its name.

Although this area was one of those most affected by 'the troubles' in Northern Ireland, the scene remains much the same today. The cement panel fencing has been replaced by iron railings. The area to the right is the City Cemetery, a Protestant burial ground in a strongly Roman Catholic part of the city, which suffered greatly from vandalism over the years. Although the new fence is to protect the cemetery from intruders, the spikes are pointed inwards as if to prevent people escaping. This has not been identified as a major problem! *Robert Mack*

Left Belfast trolleybuses front and back! Both vehicles are BUT 941s, 228 and 229 (OZ 7330 and OZ 7331), with GEC electrical equipment and 68-seater Harkness bodywork, and they are seen at the corner of Whiterock Road and Springfield Road on 29 March 1967. No 229 is heading for the terminus, which was a few yards down Springfield Road at Divismore Crescent, while 228 is returning to the city centre with an incorrect destination display.

The last batch of 24 BUTs (211 to 234) was fitted with twin-track route number blinds, the reasons being first that there was considerably less winding required by the platform crews, and second the linen needed for a single-track blind with numbers from 1 to 99 would have been almost 40 metres long, while twin-track blinds required less than one-fifth of that.

The area has changed very little in the intervening years, although the 'Give Way' signs have given way to traffic lights, protected by a wire cage as a defence against stone-throwers. *E. M. H. Humphreys*

Above This view was taken on the very wet 'last day', 12 May 1968. BUT 179 (GZ 8543) heads two other trolleybuses at Whiterock terminus, the last one of which is 112. Several enthusiasts are hovering about striving to get the best pictures in a part of Belfast that was to become known throughout the world as one of the main areas of Republican terrorism - Ballymurphy. It is noteworthy that not only had the route number become 11 by 1962, but also the turning circle had been re-wired to allow vehicles to turn in a clockwise direction, as a matter of operational safety. The area is little different today. *Robin Symons*

Right When this photograph was taken in the 1960s, Belfast was enjoying one of its most peaceful periods when the main concern of many people was the cost of living and whether television would sound the death knell for the local cinemas. Whiterock was the last major trolleybus route opened in Belfast. In fact, the decision to replace

motor buses with trolleys on the Whiterock Road was taken only four days before the decision was taken in principle to abandon trolleybuses altogether! Part of the reason for converting Whiterock to trolleybuses was that quite a lot of surplus overhead wiring equipment was recovered from the closure of the Holywood Road and Ormeau Road routes, and part was that it made more sense politically to operate the Whiterock route as part of the Falls Road group of services than as part of the Donegall Road motor bus route, as had been the case, having regard to the demographic realities of the time.

At the time of this photograph the trolleybuses used the turning circle in an anti-clockwise direction and the route number was 45. When the direction was later reversed for safety reasons, the

route number became 11, which fitted more logically into the 'Falls' group of: 11 Whiterock; 12 Falls Road; 13 Glen Road; 14 Falls Park; and 15 City Cemetery.

The side panel advertisement on AEC 48 (FZ 7833) for Park Drive cigarettes, extolling the genuine taste of good tobacco, refers to a product that is still manufactured but which has lost a considerable portion of its market share. The houses round the turning circle have changed only superficially. Originally built as public authority housing by Belfast Corporation in the early 1950s, they were taken over by the Northern Ireland Housing Executive in the early 1970s and offered for sale to their tenants in the 1980s. The main improvements visible today are the individualised front doors and double glazing. *Robert Mack*

THE NORTHERN routes were the last major group to be converted. The complex route to Glengormley changed from trams to trolleybuses in 1949, with both the Carlisle Circus and Duncairn Gardens 'legs' opening simultaneously. Turning points were established at Carlisle Circus and Strathmore Park with another at Bellevue added later. From the beginning equal frequencies were operated on both legs, with odd-numbered routes going via Carlisle Circus and even ones by way of Duncairn Gardens.

In 1950 the Greencastle tram route was withdrawn and replaced with trolleybuses, which operated about half a mile further along the Shore Road to Merville Garden Village, a short distance outside the Belfast Transport Area (BTA). A dispute with the Ulster Transport Authority (UTA) resulted in Belfast trolleybuses being unable to pick up or set down passengers along the last quarter-mile of the route. Although the matter was finally resolved by a revenue-sharing agreement between the two operators, Belfast Corporation decided to replace the trolleybuses as soon as possible and the Greencastle

route was converted to motor buses in 1962. The buses were diverted to a new terminus on the Mill Road within the BTA.

In 1951 trolleybuses replaced buses on the Cliftonville Road and the route was extended along Oldpark Road and Ballysillan Road to a turning circle at Joanmount Gardens; this terminus was known as 'Carr's Glen' after a local river. An intermediate turning circle was provided at the former tram terminus at Cliftonville Circus and trolleybuses turning there carried 'CLIFTONVILLE' on their destination screens. A siding was built near Cliftonville football ground.

Meanwhile in 1953 a branch had been established along the Whitewell Road to a turning circle at the entrance to the Throne hospital. The route was entirely inside the BTA and lasted until the end of trolleybus operation in 1968.

Turning circles were provided at Grove Park and Fortwilliam and there were sidings at Crusaders football ground and the Northern Counties Railway station.

Although this trolleybus is too far away from the camera to identify it properly, the main reason for including this picture is to illustrate the complexity of the overhead wiring at the busy junction of Upper Donegall Street (ahead), Royal Avenue (left) and York Street (right); the cameraman is standing in the mouth of Lower Donegall Street.

In June 1964, when this photograph was taken, trolleybuses operated from Royal Avenue to Whitewell via York Street, and to Carr's Glen via Upper Donegall Street. Vehicles from Lower Donegall Street served Glengormley via Upper Donegall Street and York Street. Additionally there was the facility to turn left from Lower Donegall Street into Royal Avenue. This last

manoeuvre was mainly used by trolleybuses going to and from the depot.

Turner's fruit market at 140 Royal Avenue (extreme left) and Duffin's men's shop at 144, together with the offices on the floors above, collectively known as Rea's Buildings, have since been demolished and replaced with a major extension to the *Belfast Telegraph* offices. St Patrick's Roman Catholic Church (with the spire) in the centre background, the *Irish News* offices, Donegall Street Congregational Church and Woodhouse's furniture shop are all still standing, albeit with modifications; the Woodhouse (originally Berris) building is now empty and up for sale. *John Gillham*

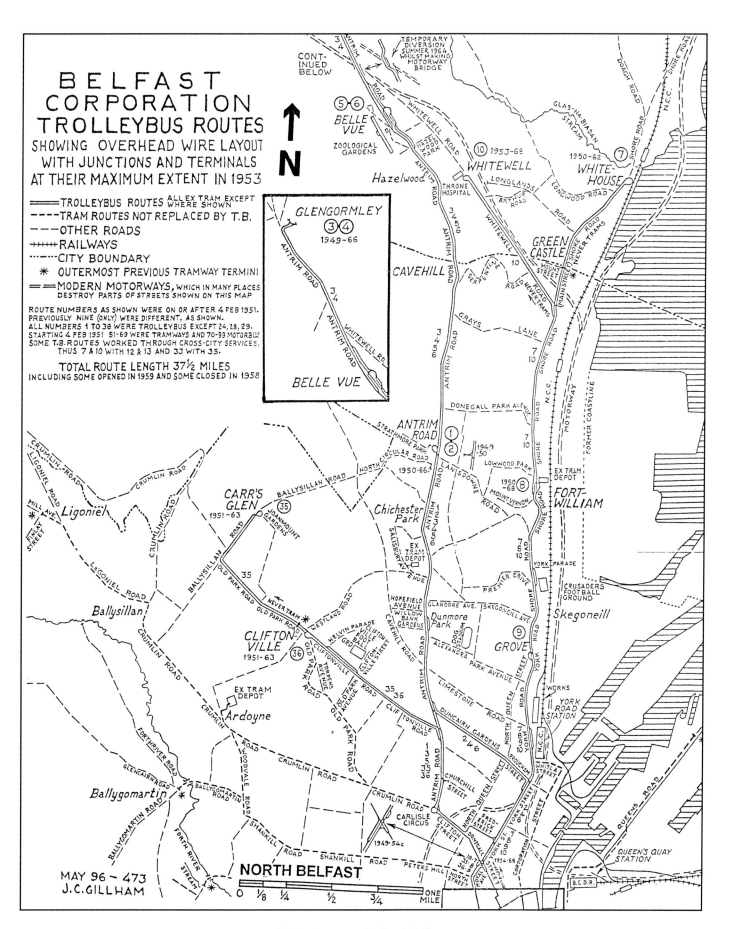

Trolleybus routes in North Belfast.

Above We are now in Carlisle Circus, looking down Clifton Street, from which BUT 192 (GZ 8556) is emerging, towards the city centre. On the left is ex-London Transport Daimler 452 (GXE 490), one of the 100 wartime Daimlers bought in 1953 and rebodied by Harkness over the following few years. Although outwardly similar to the other Harkness-bodied buses, the ex-London vehicles could be recognised by the one-piece rear window in the upper saloon; all others had two-piece windows.

The church on the right was Carlisle Memorial Methodist, a handsome edifice with a large Church Hall. It was constructed in 1875 by James Carlisle, a Belfast builder, in memory of his son. Today it is used by the Asian community, the local Methodists having moved away from the area as a result of intimidation, redevelopment and demographic change. The church in the centre background is St Patrick's Roman Catholic Church and Schools, which served the nearby New Lodge Road area. That on the left is St Enoch's Presbyterian, now replaced by a much smaller modern building serving the combined congregations of St Enoch's and Duncairn.

The area is very different today with a traffic underpass just about where the 'School' sign is at the end of the block of four-storey terraced houses. The Circus itself shows the line of the former tram track clearly; when the roundabout was recently excavated several pieces of track were uncovered. Between the bus and trolleybus is TZ 4106, a Triumph Herald. *Colin Routh*

Left Another view of Carlisle Circus showing BUT 192 (GZ 8556) en route for Carr's Glen via Cliftonville Road in the mid-1960s. No 192 is beautifully turned out, and advertising Black & White whiskey, the symbol of which was black and white cats sitting side by side. The church glimpsed on the left is St Enoch's Presbyterian and the church hall is in the centre background. The row of shops on Clifton Street, comprising the newsagent and tobacconists, Carlisle Circus Post Office and Molly Cochrane's draper's shop, is still there, although the businesses themselves have changed hands and the shops have been sympathetically refurbished. *R. F. Mack*

BELFAST TROLLEYBUSES 1938-1968

Above The turning circle at Carlisle Circus was unique in Belfast in that it allowed trolleybuses to reverse in either direction. It was not often used to turn vehicles from the city centre direction, but in the days when Bellevue and the Zoo were popular holiday attractions for Belfast families, a service of trolleybuses was operated from Carlisle Circus to Glengormley in addition to the 'regular' service from Castle Junction, essentially to allow Antrim Road passengers to make local journeys when the 'regular' service buses were full.

Roy Brook took this photograph of AEC 52 (FZ 7837) in August 1952 emerging from Antrim Road and returning to Castle Junction. The advertisement along the side for Caproni's of Bangor 'for Saturday night dancing' referred to a very popular dance hall in the seaside town of that name, about 12 miles outside Belfast. In addition to the ballroom at Ballyholme, Caproni's (or Caps) was justly famous for fish and chips and delicious home-made ice-cream. Somehow the three seemed to go well together when you were a teenager in those days.

As may be seen from the tram tracks veering to the left, trams still operated up Crumlin Road to Ligoniel when this photograph was taken, while the disconnected tracks to the right served the Antrim Road before conversion to trolleybuses in 1949. The gable to the right belonged to the Ulster Bank, and the ecclesiastical building is again St Enoch's Presbyterian Church. *Roy Brook*

Above right The Antrim Road route was most generously provided with turning facilities for trolleybuses. From the city centre these were at Carlisle Circus (turning circle in both directions); Churchill Street (reverser); Strathmore Park (turning circle); Bellevue (turning circle); and the terminus at Glengormley (reverser). In addition a reverser was provided at the York Street/Frederick Street junction, which served trolleybuses from

Duncairn Gardens. Probably the least used of these was the 'Carr's Glen' reverser at Churchill Street, the main purpose of which was to allow trolleybuses from the Antrim Road routes to reverse when the Twelfth of July procession blocked Clifton Street for a few hours.

In the early 1960s AEC 76 has just reversed into Churchill Street from the Antrim Road and is about to return to Carr's Glen. It was into this street that the trolleybus referred to in the Introduction went while trying to avoid the breakdown crew. McDonagh's chemist shop, whose gable wall can be seen on the extreme left, Morgan's warehouse on the right and all the houses in the street have been swept away. The left-hand side of the street has been redeveloped with low-rise red-brick houses, while there is a car park on waste ground on the other side. The three parked cars are an Austin 7, an Austin A35 and an Austin A40. *William Montgomery*

Above Further down the Antrim Road towards the terminus, BUT 226 (OZ 7328) was also en route to Cregagh when photographed in the early 1960s. The single deck bus behind it, A 8581 (GZ 7649), a Leyland PS1 with 34-seater NIRTB bodywork, belonged to the UTA and was returning to Belfast from Cookstown via Magherafelt on the 110 service. It was new in 1947 and lasted in service until 1966.

The pub, partly obscured by the trolleybus, was owned by P. McLaughlin and stood guard at the corner of Halliday's Road for many years. On the other side of Halliday's Road is Belfast Wine House, recognisable by its oval advertisement for Sandeman's port. The building next door was formerly the Lyceum cinema with

850 seats. Opened in 1916, it closed in 1966 when it became the Rank film depot. Unfortunately this fine building was destroyed by a terrorist bomb in 1970. *Robert Mack*

Below This view was taken on 25 February 1996 from almost the same spot. The reference points are the 'Old Bushmills' pub, the row of shops beyond the bar and the kerb line on the left-hand side of the road. The former Lyceum cinema has been demolished, as has the row of houses to its left. Redevelopment at the entrance to Halliday's Road has resulted in the openness of the junction with the Antrim Road becoming much 'tighter'. One of the considerations in this design was the security of the area. *Mike Maybin*

Above The precise date of this photograph is not known, but it was almost certainly taken during the early 1960s, shortly before the Carr's Glen to Cregagh cross-town route closed. BUT 212 (OZ 7314) is joining the Antrim Road from Cliftonville Road; from the lack of traffic and other activity it could well have been a Sunday. It was only the later batch of BUTs that were provided with a sliding cab door, which was a great boon in hot weather; those of all other Belfast trolleybuses opened outwards and the only ventilation was by the windows. The 'Sssschweppessss' theme carried on the upper deck side panel was carried right through into television commercials until quite recently.

The group of shops on the Antrim Road is interesting. The Phoenix bar (almost invisible behind the trolleybus) was where a runaway tram crashed on its uncontrolled journey from Cliftonville terminus on 12 February 1946. Reg Ludgate and Bob Hunter, in their excellent book *Gone but not Forgotten*, show a delightful picture entitled 'A Thirsty Chamberlain!', which was a reference to the type of tram involved. Of the other shops in the photograph, McLaughlin's is currently being rebuilt; Henry's has become an employment agency; and Parker's is currently a Pizzeria. *Colin Routh*

Above right This is a rather shadowy view of AEC 50 (FZ 7835), heading out of the city on Cliftonville Road, with the sun behind. The unpainted section of waist panel is clearly visible here, as is the bamboo pole and hook for the retrieval of recalcitrant trolley booms. In the early destination blinds, as fitted to the AECs, several destinations were displayed on two lines, the second one

offering more information. 'CARR'S GLEN VIA CLIFTONVILLE ROAD' is one example, but others were 'PARLIAMENT BUILDINGS [STORMONT]' and 'SHORT STRAND [ALBERT BRIDGE]'.

The Corporation erected the siding on the 'into-town' side of Cliftonville Road to allow trolleybuses to 'park' near Cliftonville football ground while awaiting the rush of spectators after the match. Thomson's shop at the corner of Cliftonville Street on the left is now Clifton Pet Supplies, and the house to its immediate left is derelict and boarded up. Parked outside is one of the hugely popular Volkswagen 'Beetles'. *Robert Mack*

In the early 1960s, AEC 48 (FZ 7833) has just turned left from Ballysillan Road into Oldpark Road. Similar to all the AECs in the batch 15-102, this vehicle was supplied with GEC electrical equipment and Harkness 68-seater body. Although the trolleybus had given about 20 years' service when this photograph was taken, it looks remarkably well turned out. The old-style 'Slow - Major Road Ahead' sign and the gas-lit swan-neck junction light in the mouth of Benview Park were still common sights in the Belfast of the 1960s.

Today the junction is controlled by traffic lights, the Lobitos garage has disappeared and the shops behind it now face the widened Ballysillan Road. The mountains remain largely unchanged, while the houses to the right and the pillars and fence around Holy Trinity Parish Church are also still there. *Robert Mack/Mike Maybin*

Right Carr's Glen terminus was located at the junction of Joanmount Gardens and Ballysillan Road, and was shared by Carr's Glen (via Cliftonville Road) trolleybuses, and Carr's Glen (via Oldpark Road) and Carr's Glen (via Cavehill Road) motor buses. Because of the awkward camber of the turning circle, passengers were not allowed to remain on the vehicles during the turning manoeuvre, as stated on the plate below the old style 'BUS STAGE' sign on the left.

Guy 115 (FZ 7900) is about to depart for Cregagh in the mid-1960s. The motor bus, 365 (OZ 6619), is a Daimler COG 6 with Harkness 56-seater bodywork, which was bought new by the Corporation in 1953 to expedite the tram replacement programme. It is working through to Ormeau Road via Great Victoria Street and Botanic Avenue. Eglinton Presbyterian Church can just be glimpsed between the two buses, and the bridge over Carr's Glen River is just

beyond the turning circle. The camera is pointing in the direction of Antrim Road and the city centre is roughly to the right. The mountain in the background is Cave Hill. *Robert Mack*

Below This unusual view of BUT 223 (OZ 7325), taken by Robin Symons from an upstairs window of 414 Antrim Road on 20 April 1965, gives a clear idea of the roof-mounted equipment of a typical trolleybus, including the duckboard and catwalk, and the trolleys mounted on large brackets. The latter were necessary to take both the weight of the trolley booms and the strain caused by the vehicle weaving from side to side. The hooks at the back were to secure the trolley booms when out of use, for example to allow another vehicle to pass or when the bus was in the depot for repair.

From left to right the shops in the picture were Magill's confectionery shop (known simply as 'the sweetie shop' by the local children), Fortwilliam Post Office, Parkes grocery store, Diamond's, and 'Maison d'Elégance' hair stylist (known as the women's hairdressers). Today Magill's still sells confectionery, the post office still sells stamps, although it has moved next door, and Diamond's has become Duncairn Wine Shop. The Bank of Ireland (successor to the Provincial) completely demolished the end house in the terrace and built a new edifice totally unsympathetic to its location. The Morris Traveller estate parked in front of the shops was often referred to as a 'shooting brake' in the 1960s, and the other cars heading out of town are a Jaguar and a Singer. *Robin Symons*

Left When the Glengormley route was converted from trams to trolleybuses in 1949, the General Manager, Col McCreary, experienced some difficulty in obtaining a suitable site for a turning circle near to where the trams' cross-over had been. Initially he had hoped to make a one-way loop using Strathmore Park and North Circular Road, but the residents vehemently objected and in the meantime he had to make do with a reversing triangle.

An unidentified Guy is seen using the triangle in 1949 or early 1950. In February of the latter year a turning circle was built on the wasteland to the right of the trolleybus next to the former Belfast Castle gate lodge. The view today is of a modern three-storey apartment building on the left and the turning circle built on the wasteground to the right. *The Deputy Keeper, Public Record Office for Northern Ireland*

Below The Antrim Road turning circle had been constructed by the date of this photograph taken in 1965. This view of Guy 106 (FZ 7891) and BUT 224 (OZ 7326) shows that the former gate lodge to Belfast Castle still stands, but the new housing estate of Strathmore Park has somewhat distorted the relationship of the lodge to the Castle.

Most of Belfast's turning circles - both bus and trolleybus - were paved with square setts. Millions were lifted as the tram tracks were removed, and they provided a cheap and effective source of paving for turning circles. Trolleybuses, in wet weather in particular, made a very distinctive sound as the rubber tyres 'squelched' around the often tight curves. Today the bus stop sign has gone and there is an ornamental design made of square setts in the centre of the turning circle. The setts are still used for paving and the Belfast Castle lodge in the background is now a dental surgery. *Robin Symons*

BELFAST TROLLEYBUSES 1938-1968

Above BUT 214 (OZ 7316) is returning to Castle Junction from Glengormley in the 1960s, and the location is the Antrim Road at Strathmore Park, with the camera pointing towards the terminus. The exit wires from the turning circle can be seen, together with the Castle gate lodge, complete with the Belfast coat-of-arms on the gable end.

An Ulster Transport Authority (UTA) bus stop sign can be seen two traction poles further up on the right; the letters were green on a white background.

The 'Belfast Castle' sign was erected following complaints that the entrance to the Castle had been somewhat obscured by the Strathmore Park housing estate. More recently the entrance has been moved to Innisfayle Park, and the Belfast Corporation sign has been replaced by a standard brown heritage sign. Otherwise the area is generally unchanged today. *Robert Mack*

Below Parts of the Antrim Road were very rural in the mid-1960s when this photograph was taken, and indeed some still are. Somewhere between Bellevue and the turning circle at Strathmore Park, Guy 168 (GZ 8532) is bound for Castle Junction. Today 168 is in the care of the National Trolleybus Association and is one of five preserved Belfast trolleybuses. *Robert Mack*

Above A rear view of BUT 191 (GZ 8555) at 'The Zoo' stop in April 1965. The Antrim Road was very narrow at this point and the retaining wall at Bellevue had to be recessed to make room for a trolleybus stop. The attractive young lady alighting from 191 looks as though she is dressed for a cold day. The traction pole ahead of the bus is located behind the wall and the one behind it carrying the 'Bus Stop' sign is equipped with the handle to change the overhead frog for Bellevue turning circle.

The land on which Bellevue, and later the Zoo, was built came as part of the Cavehill & Whitewell Tramways when they were taken over by the Belfast Corporation before the First World War. The whole area was developed into a pleasure ground and became an attraction to Belfast families for Bank Holiday excursions. The 1940s, '50s and '60's saw tens of thousands of people flocking to Bellevue on day trips and the job of getting them there

and home again taxed the resources of the Transport Department to the limit. An extra power 'feeder' was installed near Bellevue, which could be switched in to boost the electricity supply on busy days.

The 'UC' advertisement on the back of the trolleybus was an advertisement for Ulster Creameries Ice Cream. Unfortunately this was one of many small dairies that were absorbed during a takeover - they really made excellent ice-cream! *Robin Symons*

Below North Belfast shrouded in mist provides a pleasing background for Bellevue turning circle and BUT 208 (GZ 8572). The photograph was taken by Robin Symons on 20 April 1965 and apart from a hedge around the turning circle the area is hardly changed today. Even the fence is still there, albeit rather the worse for wear! *Robin Symons*

Above Another view of the turning circle in the same month, looking towards the city. On the right is BUT 201 (GZ 8565) en route to Glengormley, with 177 (GZ 8541) and 200 (GZ 8564) in the turning circle ready for the return journey to Castle Junction. The temporary 'NO PARKING' signs on the lamp standards were erected in at times when larger numbers of trolleybuses than usual might be expected to use the turning circle - at Easter, for example. The photograph clearly shows the overhead wiring that allowed trolleybuses to enter the turning circle also from the Glengormley end. This was purely for parking purposes, as the only direction for exit was towards the city centre. The severe slope of the surrounding area may be judged from the roof levels of the nearby (two-storey) houses.

Nos 177 and 200 are both advertising McCausland's car hire - was Belfast Corporation trying to tell its paying customers something? I don't ascribe cause and effect, but Belfast buses are currently carrying only a fraction of the number of passengers carried in 1965, while McCausland's has moved from its York Street premises to much larger accommodation in Grosvenor Road. In addition it has developed a successful business based at the International Airport. *Robin Symons*

Above right An aerial view of BUT 233 (OZ 7335) on the Antrim Road beyond Belle Vue in May 1964. The M2 motorway was being constructed and a traffic diversion was in operation at the point where the new road was to pass beneath. Trolleybuses were also diverted for a period to allow the major roadworks to take place, and the overhead was temporarily carried on single bracket arms.

The tea advertised on the side panel of the trolleybus - Forster Green's - although still around is perhaps not so popular. Forster Green, the original owner of the firm, endowed the hospital that bears his name at Newtownbreda, beside the former Ormeau Road trolleybus terminus.

The Lobitos garage is now a Texaco filling station and the Spar sign is no longer displayed on the gable. The main change today, of course, is the bridge that carries the Antrim Road over the motorway. The line of the motorway is at roughly 45 degrees to the Antrim Road. *Richard Whitford*

Above Although taken from a very similar location to Roy Brook's shot of AEC 28 opposite, this view of BUT 190 (GZ 8554) shows that within about ten years the right-hand side of Antrim Road had become quite built up. However, the 'Road' was still relatively traffic free; seen here, left to right, are an Austin saloon, an ERF lorry and a Hillman Minx. Note the old-style 'School' sign on the left.

Cartmill's clothes shop is still in business, although they have extended at the side and no longer use their gable for advertising. The tower behind belonged to Glengormley Presbyterian Church (and still does), while the two-storey whitewashed building in the right background was the Police Station. It is also still there, but completely hidden behind a reinforced fence designed to withstand car bombs and rockets. *Robert Mack*

Left Guy 148 (GZ 8512) is about to overtake a Bedford lorry belonging to Anderson's Haulage Contractors of Belfast, which appears to be double-parked outside Garrett's shop. The photograph was taken in the mid-1960s just below Glengormley terminus; the overhead wires can be seen turning in to the right.

The group of shops is still there today, but Boyle's has been rebuilt into the Moghul Tandoori take-away, Garrett's is now Swift Doors and Windows, and the corner shop is a solicitor's office. *Robert Mack*

This view of AEC 28 (FZ 7813) was taken by that inveterate photographer of Belfast trams, Roy Brook, in August 1952. It is about to turn right into the reversing triangle off the Antrim Road; in fact the driver has already turned his destination blind to 'CASTLE JUNCTION' in preparation for the return trip. Glengormley had not yet been developed in the early 1950s and the rural character of the area is still very evident from this photograph; such street lighting as existed was gas-powered. The tram track has not yet been lifted, although trams had not operated to Glengormley for more than three years when this photograph was taken. The adults' style of dress, particularly the

man's long raincoat and the lady's headscarf, are rather typical of the 1950s.

Today the left-hand kerb-line and the mountain range in the background are about the only reference points between the two views. The right-hand side of the road now comprises a BP filling station, a new shopping complex known as the 'Tramways Centre' (presumably in honour of the Cavehill & Whitewell Tramway) and a branch of Iceland, the frozen food chain. The corner where the group of people was standing in 1952 is presently occupied by Hughes Insurance Brokerage. One of the current 'Citybus' stop signs can be seen on the lamp standard on the right. *Roy Brook/Mike Maybin*

Above Glengormley was the only terminus in Belfast to retain a reversing triangle throughout its life. As it was on private land the danger and inconvenience were minimised, but even so platform crews were instructed to be particularly vigilant when reversing. The long safety barrier evidences the Corporation's unease about the possibility of passengers being hurt. Roy Brook photographed AEC 17 (FZ 7802) at Glengormley in August 1952. Trolleybuses turned right from the Antrim Road into the triangle and passengers disembarked at a stop on the left. The buses then turned left into the small fenced-off cul-de-sac just about where the conductor is in the photograph, then reversed to the right into the cul-de-sac seen straight away, which was also fenced. From there they approached the stop on the right of the picture and boarded passengers for town. Alongside is a 'Youth for Christ' poster, advertising one of the great religious crusades for which Belfast was well known.

The two 'STOP' signs were from tram days. Although there were special trolleybus STOP and STAGE signs available for many years, by the early 1950s the Corporation used signs interchangeably. The subsidiary sign below the 'STAGE' reads 'QUEUE THIS SIDE OF BARRIER'. The lettering was white on a blue background.

As seen on the previous page, this area has changed significantly. The right-hand side is taken up by Hughes Insurance Brokerage and the safety fence and wooden hut have been removed. On the left-hand side there is the Shapla Tandoori house and Inshape sunbeds. *Roy Brook*

Left In the mid-1960's BUT 202 (GZ 8566) is in the second cul-de-sac and is about to take up position at the stand before returning to town. The building behind the trolleybus is Glengormley Primary School, which survives today, as does the 5th Belfast (Glengormley) Scouts' hut on the left. The wire mesh fence has been cut back a bit, but otherwise the area is quite recognisable. *Robert Mack*

Right For some reason that is not imme- diately obvious, many more photographs were taken of trolleybuses on the Carlisle Circus 'leg' of the Antrim Road routes than on the Duncairn Gardens one, but here is one of Guy 110 (FZ 7895) at the top of Duncairn Gardens near its junction with Antrim Road on 15 June 1964, about two years before the route was surren- dered to motor buses. The advertisement for the 'Welcome Pinta' was part of a major campaign by the Milk Marketing Board to promote the image of their prod- uct as healthy and economical!

On the left is the Belfast Banking Company Ltd (now owned by the Northern Bank) and a set of Belfast Corporation flats, which were built short- ly after the war to replace houses demol- ished by the Luftwaffe in 1941. Although not visible in this picture, no fewer than three churches in Duncairn Gardens were destroyed in the same raid: Duncairn Gardens Methodist, St Barnabas (Church of Ireland) and Macrory Memorial Presbyterian Churches. Today the Belfast

Bank is Creaney's shoe shop, but the fine terrace of three-storey houses further down Duncairn Gardens has fortunately not been demolished. The car behind the trolleybus is a Ford Prefect. *John Gillham*

Below BUT 195 (GZ 8560) passes the Head Office of the Belfast Co-Operative Society in York Street the 1960s. At that time the Co- Operative Movement was a major trading force in Belfast as in most working districts in the United Kingdom. This impressive building was constructed in 1931-32 by Samuel Stephenson; at five storeys high and 15 bays wide it was one of the largest department stores in the city.

The top floor was given over to Share Accounts. As already mentioned on page 31, many families had a share in 'The Co', as it was affectionately known, and received a discount (called the Dividend) on all their purchases except tobacco products. I can remember accompanying my parents to withdraw money from our account for birthdays and Christmas. There was very long

counter protected by a wire grille, along which there were access points manned by stony faced cashiers. There was a point for customers whose share number was between 1 and 10000; anoth- er for numbers in the range 10001 to 20000 and so on. I can well remember the impatience of seemingly endless queues and the bribe of a 'Coke' at the Orpheus restaurant, which was also part of the Co-Op service, which I believe also doubled as a dance hall on Saturday evenings.

The building is now a part of the University of Ulster at Belfast and is physically attached to it by a covered overhead pedestrian bridge at the seventh bay from the left - just about where the front of the trolleybus is in the photograph. Henry's Stores to the left is currently an empty site.

The Heinz advertisement on the trolleybus has changed in style from those days, but the company itself has grown considerably from the days when it marketed its '57 Varieties'. The two vehicles behind the bus are a Bedford van and a Ford Popular car. *R. F. Mack*

Although AEC 20 (FZ 7805) shows 'GLENGORMLEY' on its destination blind, it is heading towards Castle Junction in York Street on 11 August 1962. The shop on the left was the sole survivor on the right-hand side of the street of the Belfast Blitz of 1941. The two cars outside it are Fords - one a Popular and the other an Anglia - and the car park behind the trolleybus is now the University of Ulster's Belfast campus. *Denis Battams*

In tramcar days there was a very popular facility at both the Northern Counties and County Down railway stations. Trams came right into the station, under cover, and passengers were able to get to and from trains without getting wet. Unfortunately neither the Shore Road trolleybuses nor the Queen's Road motor buses replicated that excellent early version of transport integration. The trolleybuses were provided with a siding at the Northern Counties station in York Road, and this photograph shows Guy 126 (FZ 7911) parked in the station siding en route for the City Hall. The actual location of the siding was a little way north of the passenger exit and the practice was for the trolleybus to wait for the incoming train to disembark its passengers, then make its way to the stop outside the station and pick up its fares at that point. Since the overhead line had reverted to single by this stage, the operational benefit was rather limited.

BUT 201 (GZ 8565) is making for Falls Road on the outside pair of wires, followed by a Leyland PD3/4 of early 1960s vintage owned by the Ulster Transport Authority (UTA); it carries a 69-seater body completed by its owner on MCW frames. As a matter of interest this vehicle was among the last new double-deck buses bought by the UTA.

The advertisements along the side wall of the station are for the *News of the World* - 'All Human Life is There' - and Player's cigarettes. The wall, later surrounding Northern Ireland Railways' property, has now been removed and the area has been given over to Richardson's Tiles. *Robin Symons*

Right Guy 178 (GZ 8542), in Shore Road heading towards Glen Road via the city centre in the mid-1960s, has just passed a 'feeder' point, as evidenced by the steel cabinets beside the traction pole to the left of the bus and by the insulators in the overhead wire just above the church.

Samuel Getty's newsagency and sweet shop on the left was located at the corner of Shore Road and Northwood Road. In many ways it was typical of the small corner shop once so common in Belfast, and now, while not quite a thing of the past, certainly much rarer. Cigarette advertisements often identified such emporia (lovely word!) and the competing claims of Gallaher's Blues, Player's, Nelson and Park Drive are all represented here. Another phenomenon seen much less often today is the outside vending machine, and Getty's has a cigarette machine, a milk vendor and a chewing gum machine. The decline of these slot machines resulted from a combination of increased vandalism, decimalisation and rapid inflation, the last of which in particular made the vending machines uneconomic to operate because of the frequent need to alter the coin mechanism. Getty's

has now become Annie's, but still sells newspapers and tobacco, although the vending machines are long gone. The remainder of the houses in the terrace are still there, and the church behind the trolleybus is Seaview Presbyterian. *Robert Mack*

Below Guy 168 (GZ 8532) is passing the Northern Counties Railway station on York Road in the late 1960s on route 13 heading for Glen Road from Whitewell. The street on the left is Brougham Street, leading to Duncairn Gardens and the Glengormley trolleybus route. By the time this photograph was

taken the overhead wires had been dismantled following the closure of that route in 1966.

The public house on the corner (Woods Bros) is advertising White Horse whisky, Bass beer and, below the corner window, 'Gallaher's Tipped in the Red Pack'. In the right background one of the ex-London Transport Daimler buses is working the cross-town Downview Avenue to Ormeau via Cromac Street service. It is perhaps surprising that in the late 1960s gas lighting persisted at road junctions, both in the swan-neck lamp and inside the 'Keep Left' signs - and this despite the electric lights on the main road! *Robert Mack*

Right The Blitz of 1941 caused a great deal of damage to a number of areas in Belfast. Not only did Harland & Wolff's shipyard and Short & Harland's aircraft factory suffer much more destruction than was admitted at the time, but many houses in North Belfast were razed to the ground. As a temporary expedient, Belfast Corporation built pre-fabricated dwelling units ('pre-fabs') on several sites, including here in Shore Road. As so often happens, the pre-fabs lasted much longer than planned and clearance had just begun when this photograph was taken by Ed Humphreys in April 1966.

The trolleybus is Guy 127 (FZ 7912), with GEC electrical equipment and Harkness 68-seater bodywork, on the cross-town Whitewell to Falls Road service. It went into service in 1948 and lasted until the end of trolleybus operation in 1968.

Heinz's advertisements in the 1950s and '60s tended to stress the huge number of 'varieties' (57), until it was realised that the company produced many hundreds of different products! This advertisement for the company's staple and probably best-known product ('Beanz') graced the sides of many Belfast public service vehicles for a number of years. The building in the distance with the large advertising hoarding is the end of a row of terrace houses originally known as 'Depot Terrace' in honour of the tram depot, visible to the right of the hoarding and still standing today. The vacant ground in front of the pre-fabs has become football pitches known as Loughside Playing Fields, and the pre-fabs themselves have given way (eventually) to Loughside Recreation Centre. The two cars nearest the camera are the rear view of a Triumph Herald and the front view of a Morris Minor. *E. M. H. Humphreys*

Below When the trolleybus service opened on Shore Road in

1950 a turning circle was established on land near Shore Road tram depot, and the 'parallel' wires leading into the turning circle can be seen on the left of this picture of BUT 196 (GZ 8560). Like all the first BUT batch, 196 was fitted with GEC electrical equipment and Harkness 68-seater double-deck body. However, unlike most of its sisters it did not survive until 1968 - the year of closure - but perished in a fire in Falls Road Depot in 1966.

The single-storey brick building on the extreme left of the picture belonged to T. B. F. Thompson of Garvagh, who held the agency for Morris cars when this photograph was taken in the mid-1960s; they also sold BP petrol. Squeezed in beside was H. Hutton's builders suppliers. The garage business is no longer there, but Hutton's were still in the tile business - at least until recently. Their premises appear to be derelict at present. *Robert Mack*

Above Initially a 3-minute service was provided between Castle Junction and Fortwilliam turning circle throughout the day, with every second vehicle being projected to Whitehouse. At the peak periods of morning, lunchtime and evening, all vehicles served the Whitehouse terminus on a 3-minute frequency. Here BUTs 222 (left) and 220 (OZ 7324 and OZ 7322) are seen at Fortwilliam in March 1967; 222 is en route from Whitewell to Glen Road while her sister is bound for the Falls Road, having completed a short working to Fortwilliam.

The terminus was designed with a parallel set of wires leading into the turning circle, just visible on the left of the picture. This arrangement allowed a trolleybus bound for Fortwilliam to take up a position just to the left of the centre line of the road and await a break in the oncoming traffic while a Whitewell vehicle could pass it on the inside. The Land Rover may well have belonged to an Inspector from the traffic department.

The building to the right of the Bass advertisement is the former Shore Road tram depot and is still standing today, albeit as a Northern Ireland Electricity sub-station. The houses on the left are little changed, although the Mini heading out of town has probably been scrapped many years ago. The houses in the centre are also still standing, though derelict. The turning circle has been landscaped. *E. M. H. Humphreys*

Below This view of AEC 85 (FZ 7870) about to return to Haymarket Depot from Whitewell terminus was taken on the same day as the one above, and the rural character of the terminus is readily evident. The general view today shows the roofs of new houses in the valley below the terminus, but otherwise there is no change from when this photograph was taken. 'Ediswan' lamps and electronic components is a name from the past. *Stan Letts*

Left Guy 177 (GZ 8541) leaves Whitewell terminus on its way to the Falls Road on 11 August 1962; an unidentified trolley-bus stands in the turning circle. The Whitewell route was one of the later additions to the network, being opened in 1953. The overhead wiring was equipped with curved 'segments' that reduced the number of 'pull-offs' required and presented a smoother curve to the trolley heads.

The brick building in the background was the Throne hospital; it has since been decommissioned and is currently for sale. *Denis Battams*

Below Back on Shore Road near its junction with Whitewell Road, AEC 68 (FZ 7853) passes in the early 1960s. When trolleybuses first replaced trams on Shore Road, they were linked with the Falls Road route and 68 is on its way there. The 'via' screen shows 'VIA YORK STREET, CASTLE STREET AND FALLS ROAD', which was the correct sequence of thoroughfares for the Whitehouse to Falls Road direction, but trolleybuses travelling the opposite way also showed the same display, which gave rise to confusion to more than one stranger! The side panel advertisement for Black and White whisky promotes a product that has lost nothing of its popularity in the succeeding 30 years.

The shop sign for Wills's Capstan cigarettes is long since gone, as is John Harper's grocery shop at number 858 and Brown's cosmetics at 862. Incidentally, Shore Road contained the highest numbered house (1211) in Belfast, followed by Crumlin Road, where the numbers reached 1010a. The area has changed radically since the date of this photograph; the buildings between the Harlequin cake van and the trolleybus have been replaced by modern single-storey shops, while the shops to the right of the picture have also been removed and the area given over to grass around the M2 motorway, one access to which is now located approximately where the row of shops is behind the trolleybus. *Robert Mack*

This photograph was taken in Shore Road precisely on the city boundary (or at least where the boundary was prior to the 1973 revision). The old boundary post can be seen on the right together with the large square sign with its back to the camera, which was the decorative 'City of Belfast' sign. The difference in the road surface is quite obvious; Belfast Corporation has its white lines clearly painted, but Antrim County Council had yet to mark theirs out. The slightly different road width is also evident at the division between the local authorities. Guy 174 (GZ 8538) is en route to Falls Road in the early 1960s (the route number 12 suggests this, although the destination blind is half way between).

The former tram terminus at Greencastle was exactly on the boundary, close to Mount Street. Greaves's Mill rises in the background, while the little houses to the right emphasise the rural nature of this area, even in the early 1960s.

The area is barely recognisable in February 1996. The cottages on the left have been demolished, although the railings that originally surrounded them are still there, as is the rather squat flat-roofed, two-storey building beyond. The mill has also gone, as have the more substantial houses further along the road and all the small houses on the right. To the right, just out of sight of the camera, is a major motorway junction today. *Robert Mack/Mike Maybin*

Above An off-side view of Guy 184 (GZ 8548) as it is about to turn right into the turning circle at Whitehouse. By the time that this photograph was taken in early 1962, shortly before the route was converted to motor bus operation, all trolleybuses had been fitted with flashing direction indicator lights. The side panel advertisement for (Player's) Gold Leaf promotes a brand of cigarettes no longer available. In the 1960s Gallaher's factories in Belfast and Ballymena were major sources of employment and a commercial rival to Player's.

Today the turning circle itself has been removed, but the houses in the background are still there. The car behind the trolleybus is a Ford Anglia. *Colin Routh*

Left Whitehouse terminus was one of the larger turning circles in Belfast and easily held eight trolleybuses. For more than a year there was a dispute between Belfast Corporation and the Ulster Transport Authority about the carriage of passengers in this area, during which passengers were allowed neither to board nor alight at the turning circle. AEC 28 (FZ 7813) awaits custom in the early 1960's. McKenna & McGinley's 'Model Orange' was produced in their model factory in Bath Place off Divis Street in the Lower Falls. Sadly they no longer trade from there.

The turning circle itself disappeared a number of years ago, but otherwise the area has not changed greatly. *Colin Routh, courtesy of Andrew Bronn*

Falls Depot

Known variously as Falls Road, Falls Park or more often just plain 'Falls', the depot is located at the junction of Falls and Glen Roads in West Belfast and is next door to a large public park. It was originally opened as a horse tram depot in 1886 and shortly after its opening was the scene of a pitched battle between supporters and opponents of the Home Rule Bill.

It was converted to accommodate the electric cars in 1905 and in 1926 became the Corporation's first bus garage. However, with the expansion of the bus fleet in the 1930s a proportion of the tramcar fleet was relocated to other depots.

In 1938 the 14 new trolleybuses were housed in Falls Depot and the remaining tramcars transferred elsewhere. In 1947 it became the main overhaul works for both buses and trolleybuses, and although buses continued to use it as a 'running' depot, the trolleybuses were transferred to Haymarket for operational purposes. Following the abandonment of trolleybuses in 1968 the overhead wiring was dismantled. At the time of writing (1996) the depot is still used by Citybus.

An unusual side view of T2 (EZ 7890) in the forecourt of Falls Depot at around the time of the opening of the first trolleybus service. It is an AEC 664T with English Electric electrical equipment and Harkness 68-seater bodywork. Clearly this photograph was specially posed, but is nevertheless interesting. *H. Fayle (Irish Railway Record Society)*

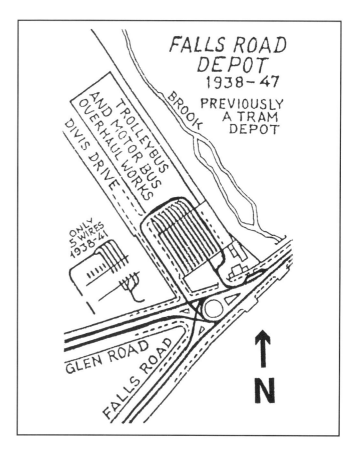

A shot of the interior of Falls Road tram depot when it had just been converted for trolleybus operation. The two main changes were the modification of the overhead wiring and the creation of an entrance for trolleybuses from Divis Drive. The pits remained in situ and their existence required very precise steering by the trolleybus drivers! The lattice roof originated in the city and became known as the 'Belfast Roof'. While cheap to construct (and remarkably solid), it was a potential fire risk, as the two fires at Falls Depot in the 1960s confirmed.

Trolleybuses AEC 2 (EZ 7890), Daimler 6 (EZ 7894) and Crossley 4 (EZ 7892) can be seen. Although a Crossley, the latter did not have the characteristic 'Crossley curves' so evident on fleet number 3; this was because Harkness built the body! Side-mounted semaphore traffic signals were initially fitted to all Belfast trolleybuses, but were replaced by the much more reliable flashing lights in the early 1960s.

The depot is still on this site, but following the fires it was extensively rebuilt and modernised. It is currently the main workshop for Citybus. *William Montgomery*

Above BUT 210 (GZ 8574) was photographed in Falls Depot in the late 1960s by David Irwin, who worked as an electrician there for many years. The vehicle has just been prepared for a return to service following a major overhaul. 'Christie's Wallpapers', advertised on the main side panel, have thrived since this photograph was taken, and now have about 14 shops. *David Irwin*

Below This view of AEC 98 (FZ 7983) taken in the forecourt of the

depot in 1963 shows the vehicle in pristine condition, just before being handed over to the Ulster Folk & Transport Museum. It was the first Belfast trolleybus to be given for preservation. When the East Belfast routes were converted to motor bus operation in 1963, all the remaining AECs (including 98) were withdrawn from service. It is interesting to compare the overhead wiring in this view with that in the 1938 view opposite - it is noticeably lighter in appearance. *David Irwin*

Haymarket Depot

When the decision was taken to replace trams with trolleybuses it was clear that Falls Depot would be unable to accommodate the entire fleet. The Transport Department therefore acquired a temporary lease on the 'Hay Market' (sic) from the Corporation Estates Department. This site was located to the south of East Bridge Street, although not easily visible from the main road. It was far from ideal, being close to an area of small terraced houses whose front doors opened directly on to the pavement and around which children played. The trolleybuses of course provided an ideal adventure playground and staff were forever chasing them from the depot. Eventually a municipal playground was built nearby but never became as popular as the trolleybus depot!

The depot was opened for trolleybus operation on 13 February 1941 and served the East Belfast routes of Cregagh, Castlereagh, Dundonald, Stormont and Bloomfield. Space quickly became short and Haymarket (now one word) was modernised and extended by May 1947.

The depot entrances and exits were always extremely awkward. Turnley Street was used in the early days for buses going to and from service, and drivers had to take extreme care, not only because the narrow street was often full of children, but also because the overhead wiring allowed little tolerance for manoeuvre. Later Stewart Street was wired for trolleybuses entering the depot, and Annette Street was similarly equipped for vehicles departing to take up service in the direction of the city centre, and this greatly eased the situation. Although Turnley Street remained wired, it was generally used only for trolleybuses turning right to head for the Albert Bridge.

Haymarket was closed for trolleybus operation on 12 May 1968. It was then used for a short period as a bus garage, but later totally demolished and is now a new housing estate.

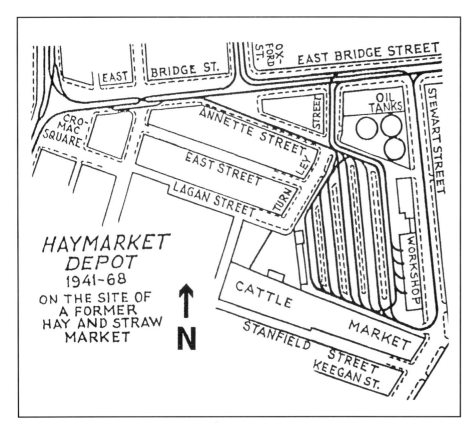

Guy 112 (FZ 7897), on a National Trolleybus Association special on the last Saturday of operation, 12 May 1968, was photographed in Stewart Street, which led to the main entrance to Haymarket Depot. The destination displays were specially made for the occasion, since 'SPECIAL' appeared only on motor bus blinds. The building behind is Belfast City Abattoir, which was opened for public use in 1913. For the ghoulish, cattle were slaughtered by the 'Cash Captive Bolt' type of gun that had the effect of simultaneously stunning the animal. The abattoir remained in operation until 28 October 1970 when it was replaced by a new plant at Duncrue Street. The area has since been completely demolished and replaced by neat one- and two-storey housing. *Robin Symons*

BELFAST TROLLEYBUSES 1938-1968

Top This is a rare side view of ex-Wolverhampton 287 (DDA 987), which was renumbered by Belfast Corporation as 237, although the registration number was retained. A Sunbeam MF2 with BTH electrical equipment and Park Royal 54-seater body, it was acquired in 1952 and withdrawn from service only two years later. Its ultimate fate is not known to me.

It is seen here in Annette Street, having just left Haymarket Depot to take up service on the 36 to Cliftonville (a short working of the Carr's Glen route). Unlike all other 'proper' Belfast Corporation trolleybuses, the Wolverhampton's retained a single destination blind at the side entrance, although the front display was modified to the Belfast standard before entering service. The ticket machine carried by the conductor is one of the new 'Ultimates' produced by the Bell Punch Company as a mechanised (and supposedly faster) version of the old Bell Punch used by almost every urban transport undertaking in the UK for more than 60 years.

'The Ulster Wine Company Ltd', whose advertisement is carried by the trolleybus, no longer trades, and all the dwellings have since been demolished and replaced by modern low-rise housing. *Andrew Bronn*

Middle A fine view of the complex overhead wiring at the Turnley Street entrance to Haymarket Depot. This was the main entrance until Stewart Street was wired in the early 1950s. Latterly Turnley Street was mainly used for trolleybuses entering service in the morning and turning right to go over the Albert Bridge bound for East Belfast routes, while Annette Street was used as the main exit from the depot.

By the time this photograph was taken in June 1964, a few diesel buses had sneaked into the depot. The nearer of the two is advertising Dulux paint, still one of the best sellers in the UK. The other is advertising Harcourt's coal; this firm continues to trade from Ballymena, and there was a Councillor Harcourt associated with Belfast Corporation for a number of years. As already mentioned, the entire area is now a housing estate. *John Gillham*

Bottom A 'full frontal' view of 4 (EZ 7892) and 11 (EZ 7899). The former was a Crossley with Metro-Vick electrical equipment and Harkness body while 11 was a Leyland TTB with GEC electrical equipment and Leyland body; both vehicles seated 68 passengers. While an accurate date is not available, the absence of a 'BELFAST CORPORATION' legend on the waist panel and the lack of a rear destination display on the bus to the left suggests that it was taken in the mid-1950s.

The photograph clearly shows the detailed differences between buses of the differing makes; the upstairs windows, downstairs windscreens, location of the side lights and the grille below the number plate are among the more obvious. *D. A. Jones (London Trolleybus Preservation Society)*

Crossley 3 (EZ 7891) photographed in Haymarket Depot by the late Henry Rea in 1951. The characteristic 'Crossley curves' are very evident in this view: the 'dip' in the leading upper deck side windows, the curve to the upstairs front windows above the destination display, and the 'droop' to the downstairs side window nearest the door can all clearly be seen.

Some time before 1957 alterations were carried out to several of the 'first 14', and the following were amongst the changes made to No 3: the route number blind was

moved from the near side to the off side, which was the standard Belfast arrangement, and both Citybus and Ulsterbus now specify route number boxes to the 'right' from the driver's view; the upper deck leading side windows were 'straightened' at the bottom; the front windows had the curve at the bottom straightened; the downstairs end window was 'straightened'; and the painting and lining were applied to the front in a straight line to de-emphasise the driver's curved windows. Mrs Cullen's Powders seem to be able to clear all sorts of illnesses from chills to nerve pains! *Henry Rea*

Henry Rea also took this rear view of, on the left, Guy 100 (FZ 7885), AEC 61 (FZ 7846) and Guy 184 (GZ 8448) in Haymarket Depot in the summer of 1951. All the trolleybuses retain their rear destination displays and 'BELFAST CORPORATION' legends along the waist panels. The Corporation later remodelled the depot and installed additional overhead wiring. Note how the pressure of two sets of trolley booms (100 and 61) has caused something of an uplift to the wires! *Henry Rea*

Left This is Sunbeam W 129 (GZ 1620) after it had been refurbished. Initially it was one of a pair of utility vehicles obtained new in 1943 at a time when public service vehicles of any description were very difficult to get, and the Corporation was in no position to be choosy. As delivered 129 was equipped with British Thompson-Houston electrical equipment and Park Royal 56-seater body. The subsequent semi-utility vehicles received in 1946 were much more comfortable and the two originals (129 and 130) were upgraded to match. It is interesting to compare this view of 129 with that on page 26. *Henry Rea*

Below Again the date of this photograph is not known, but I would guess the early 1950s, given the 'BELFAST CORPORATION' legend along the waist panels. Identifiable in the picture are, left to right, 113 (FZ 7898), 61 (FZ 7846) and 97 (FZ 7882), a Guy BTX and two AECs, all with electrical equipment by BTH and Harkness bodywork. No 97's destination screen shows 'OLDPARK', which was one of the North Belfast routes seriously considered for conversion to trolleybus operation in the late 1940s. However, when the tramcars were withdrawn, the decision was taken to substitute motor buses instead. Scribona Kemp, advertised on 61, were well known for their cakes and biscuits in the 1950s and '60s, but the name is no longer used for trading purposes. *Bristol Vintage Bus Group*

Above By the start of the 1950s the Corporation was very anxious to speed up the replacement of trams by trolleybuses, but they were unable to buy new trolleybuses as quickly as they would have liked and an opportunity presented itself to purchase 11 surplus vehicles from Wolverhampton. These were shipped over to Belfast and refurbished before entering service on Shore Road, where they spent most of their time. Their registration numbers were DDA 182 and DDA 986 to 995. While in Wolverhampton they carried the fleet numbers 282 and 286 to 295, but were renumbered 235 to 245 in the Belfast fleet.

This view of six of the ex-Wolverhampton vehicles in 'ex-works' condition was posed in 1952 in Haymarket Depot. The buses were easily recognisable as 'non-standard' by their registration numbers, the layout of the side destination display, and their having only four wheels. The gasometer providing the backdrop to the trolleybuses was demolished several years ago and Belfast has no longer a supply of coal gas. *William Montgomery*

Right As part of the upgrading of Haymarket Depot in 1947 a small corrugated iron shed with pits was built, which allowed the engineering staff to carry out routine maintenance and minor repairs. Illumination was still provided by a mixture of natural light and incandescent bulbs, fluorescent lights being some years in the future as far as Belfast Corporation was concerned. Here AEC 32 (FZ 7817) is having some work carried out in August 1962; by that date the trolleybus was 21 years old and was still due to give another year's service. *Denis Battams*

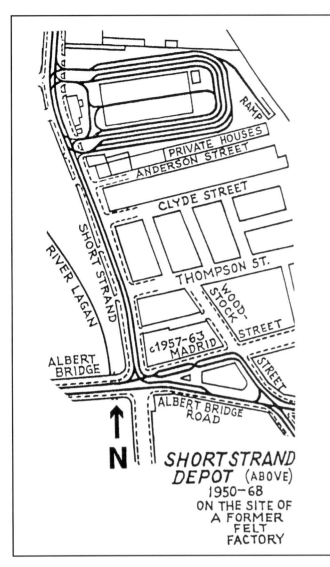

Short Strand Depot

Short Strand is, as might be expected, a short street to the east of the River Lagan linking Bridge End with Albertbridge Road and situated only a few hundred yards from two major trolleybus junctions. Although the site was acquired in 1940 specifically to house the East Belfast trolleybuses, wartime material and labour shortages prevented any development, and Haymarket was acquired as a 'stop-gap' measure. In 1947 the local firm of R. & W. Lusty cleared the old felt works from the site and Harland & Wolff erected a war-surplus aircraft hangar, which was to provide a basic covered work area for the 18 vehicle-servicing pits.

The depot opened for trolleybus operation on 2 October 1950 and later for bus operation. The capacity was 80 trolleybuses and 100 motor buses. Short Strand accommodated most of the vehicles serving East Belfast, while Haymarket also served the new North Belfast routes of Glengormley, Shore Road and Carr's Glen.

Proposals

There were only three trolleybus depots in Belfast, but in 1951 a plan was prepared that considered converting Ardoyne Depot to accommodate trolleybuses in the event that the proposals to convert Ligoniel, Ballygomartin and Oldpark tram routes to trolleybuses was put into operation. Sandy Row Depot was used in the early 1950s to store trolleybus chassis, while Knock Depot was used for a short period in the late 1950s to store the withdrawn ex-Wolverhampton trolleybuses. None of these depots was ever wired for trolleybuses.

In the late 1940s a depot was proposed for the Windsor area, which would have probably accommodated trolleybuses, but a decline in the number of passengers carried since 1948 effectively killed the scheme.

Guy 112 (FZ 7897) is about to turn right from Short Strand into the depot on the last day of operation, Sunday 12 May 1968; the destination displays of 'SPECIAL' and 'NTA TOUR' were specially made for the occasion.

When Short Stand Depot was first opened for trolleybuses in the early 1950s the street from which it took its name linked Bridge End and Albertbridge Road, and the overhead wiring at both junctions was complex. Trolleybuses were able to enter and leave the depot from either Albert Bridge or Bridge End directions. However, by 1968 the wiring had been reduced to a single pair of wires in and out from the Albert Bridge direction only. By that time the depot was used only for repairs and servicing as Haymarket was the only operating depot left. The area has undergone considerable redevelopment and is barely recognisable today.
E. M. H. Humphreys

Right Fleet No 7 (EZ 7895), a Guy BTX with English Electric electrical equipment and Park Royal bodywork, stands in Short Strand Depot in the late 1950s. When first delivered, 7 had its front route number box located on the near side; however, following representations from the union it was moved to the off side and this became the standard for Belfast.

The advertisements for McEwan's beer, Kemp's biscuits and 'Player's Please' are typical of those found on many Belfast trolleybuses of the time. Of the three products advertised, only Kemp's biscuits have gone out of production in the intervening 30 years or so. *D. A. Jones (London Trolleybus Preservation Society)*

Below This view of Short Strand Depot in the 1950s shows 140 (GZ 2811), a semi-utility Sunbeam W with British Thompson-Houston electrical equipment and Harkness 56-seater bodywork, at the head of a line of trolleybuses. On the left are 191 (GZ 8555), a BUT; 177 (GZ 8541) a Guy BTX; and, behind, 152 (GZ 8516), also a Guy from the same batch. On the right are 379 (OZ 6633) and 369 (OZ 6623), both of which were part of the batch of 100 Daimler CVG6 motorbuses bought in 1952 to speed up the tram replacement programme. They were fitted with Gardner six-valve engines and Harkness 56-seater bodies.

The destination display on 191 shows 'SHORT STRAND (ALBERT BRIDGE)', which was used by trolleybuses from that direction; the equivalent from the Queen's Bridge side was 'BRIDGE END'. The lower blind on 140 shows 'VIA YORK STREET & BRIDGE STREET', a display never used in service as Bridge Street was only wired in the 'outward' direction!

Short Strand Depot is still used by Citybus, although the large metal gates on Short Strand itself have been replaced by a brick wall and the entrance transferred to a much-remodelled Mountpottinger Road. *Photographer unknown, Charles Wilson collection*

The public service regulations did not apply to trolleybuses in Northern Ireland, but the Corporation applied the same rigorous standards on a voluntary basis. This included the 'Tilt Test', which checked for stability. Although everyone protested their complete confidence in the trolleybuses, a discrete chain was applied - just in case!

This photograph was taken in Knock Depot, where the test was carried out. At that time R. Clements Lyttle, a Belfast photographic studio, carried out work for Belfast Corporation on commission. Guy 104 (FZ 7889) was in pristine condition when the photograph was taken. While the precise date is not known to me, judging by the state of tram 102 (which was withdrawn in 1946) and the dirt in the groove of the tram

track (suggesting that Knock was no longer an operational tram depot) I would guess that it was taken about 1947.

The frosted portion of the rear downstairs window allowed ladies to preserve their modesty while climbing the stairs. The large white 'T' was carried on the back of all Belfast trolleybuses to distinguish them from diesel buses and as a warning to other trolleybus drivers not to attempt to overtake.

The early trolleybuses carried destination blinds containing the names of routes that it was planned to open in the future; 'Distillery Grounds', the home of Distillery Football Club Ltd, was one. In the event it was motor buses that replaced the trams in 1952. *R. Clements Lyttle*

120   BELFAST TROLLEYBUSES 1938-1968

Unusual views

These two internal views of 246 (2206 OI), a Sunbeam F4A with BTH electrical equipment and Harkness bodywork, were taken by H. Taylor in the late 1960s.

The upstairs view (*top*) shows the grab handles fitted as standard to every new Belfast trolleybus, motor bus and tram since the 1930s, and these provided a sure path to progress along the gangway to many a person returning home after a convivial night out. The carefully angled convex mirror located at the corner of the stairwell allowed the conductor a clear view of the open platform. Although the lower saloon was fitted with a bell rope for the purpose of signalling the driver, the upper saloon was equipped only with electric bell pushes. These were red bakelite buttons mounted in a stainless steel collar upon which was engraved the words 'PUSH ONCE'. The convention in Belfast, unlike most other cities in the UK, was 'GO when stopped - one ring; STOP when going - one ring'. Two rings signalled that the bus was full and indicated to the driver not to stop to pick up passengers waiting at a stop.

The downstairs photograph shows shorter longitudinal seats than those in the photograph of T7 on page 123; 246 had only two wheels at the rear and the wheel arch was consequently shorter. The partition between the saloon and the stairs traditionally carried the fares table, but this has been removed. *H. Taylor*

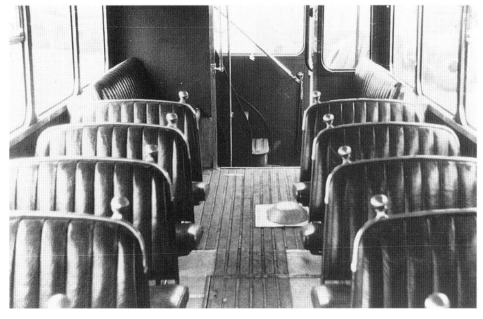

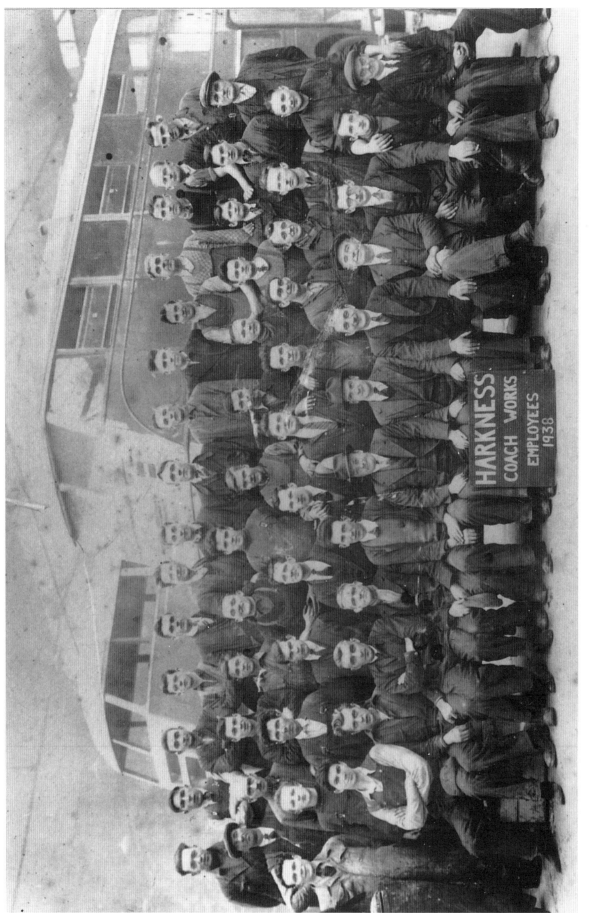

Out of the total of 246 trolleybuses that operated in Belfast between 1938 and 1968, Harkness Coachworks built the bodies for 227, or over 92 per cent. This picture, taken in the McTier Street works in 1938, shows the men who built the first Belfast trolleybuses. Among them are Willie Mackie, Coachbuilder; Dan Camplissan, Coachbuilder; Jimmy Walker, Coachbuilder; Jackie Seymour, Coachpainter; Billy Murray, Coachbuilder; Jimmy Reid, Signwriter; Sammy Seymour, Coachbuilder; Bobby Fraser, Coachbuilder; Jimmy Mackie; Coachbuilder; Robert Saunders, Sheetmetal Worker; Cecil Rodgers, Coachpainter; Jimmy Patterson, Coachbuilder;

John Girvan DD, Coachbuilder; Tommy Davidson, Sheetmetal Worker; Sammy Holmes, Coachbuilder; Albert Kirk, Coachbuilder; Isaac Harrison, Machinist; Albert Judge, Coachbuilder; Charlie Boyd, Coachbuilder; Mr Tommy Harkness and Mr James Harkness, Joint Managing Directors; George Bridges, Foreman; and Billy Harkness, Storeman.

I am very keen to identify those men not named in the photograph, so that their names can be included in any future edition of the book. I can be contacted through the publishers. *Photographer unknown, John Girvan collection.*

A photograph of the lower saloon of T7 (EZ 7895), a Guy BTX with Park Royal bodywork, taken in Park Royal Works prior to delivery to Belfast. The longitudinal seats at the back cover the wheel arches. The saloon is fitted with a clock on the front bulkhead and the electric lighting is very much a 1930s-style design. The seats were covered in Princess blue leather. *Park Royal Ltd*

This is the upstairs of 168 (GZ 8532), a Guy BTX with GEC electrical equipment and Harkness bodywork, looking towards the front. The notice reads 'FARES READY PLEASE'. There is no reference to smoking on the top deck; since the days of horse trams, Belfast Street Tramways had a 'No Smoking' policy 'inside' (or downstairs as it later was called). However, there was no objection to smoking 'outside' (or upstairs). This policy remained in force until very recently, when smoking was banned from all buses. The curved covering over the two front pillars housed the traction cables from the roof-mounted trolleypoles to the motors. *R. F. Mack*

The lower saloon of the same vehicle, again looking towards the front. It is a rather more modern-looking interior than that of T7, although there were only ten years between the two vehicles. The aluminium plate attached to the centre of the front bulkhead was for advertisement cards, and the seven horizontal bars across the lower part of the bulkhead was an attempt to protect the covering from lounging (or lunging) feet. The notices read 'FARES READY PLEASE' on the left and 'NO SMOKING' on the right. *R. F. Mack*

Above No 246 (2206 OI) is en route to preservation with the London Trolleybus Preservation Society, suspended in mid-air preparatory to being shipped 'across the water'. *John Price (London Trolleybus Preservation Society)*

Below The majority of Belfast trolleybuses were sold for scrap when the system closed in 1968, although several found a further lease of life as hen-houses and the like. BUT 211 (OZ 7313) has ended up in Beattie's scrapyard near Hillsborough, and will be broken up to allow the recovery of whatever metal is worth salvaging. *William Montgomery*

A rear three-quarter view of Guy BTX 7 (EZ 7895) with electrical equipment by English Electric and bodywork by Park Royal. The legal lettering below the number plate on the back (soon to be moved to the front near side) reads: 'SEATING CAPACITY 68, LOWER SALOON 32 UPPER SALOON 36'. The vehicle had not entered service when this photograph was taken early in 1938, and the trolley heads had not yet been fitted.

When the trolleybuses were new they were beautifully lined out in gold and black. The roof had small gutters at the edges that curved down below the rear windows, and there were two down-pipes on each side, one just behind the driver's door at the front and the other just behind the rear wheel arch at the back.

All buses were required to have emergency exits in the event that they overturned and the normal exit route was blocked. If a bus landed on its right side, it was relatively easy to escape through the regular opening at the back. If, however, the bus fell the other way, the 'cut out' at the rear panel provided an emergency escape. All Belfast double-deckers were also fitted with an emergency escape route through the rear upstairs window that could be opened from either side. *Park Royal Ltd*

Tower wagons

Left This photograph was taken in late 1948 on the Antrim Road and shows the trolleybus overhead wiring being erected for the service that began in January 1949. The tram is Standard Red 198, one of a batch of 63 built by the Corporation in Sandy Row between about 1908 and about 1916.

The tower wagon began life as a Leyland PLSC1 bus with a Leyland 31-seater single-deck body initially owned by HMS *Catherwood* of Belfast. It was bought in 1927 to compete with the railways and when the bus war began in Belfast in 1928 it was switched to the city to compete with the trams. Following the settlement between the private owners and the Corporation in December 1928, XI 9102 was taken over by the newly formed Tramways & Motors Department and became No 19 in the Corporation fleet. It was later converted to a tower wagon and renumbered TW 13. It was finally withdrawn from service in January 1949. *Robert O'Sullivan*

Below This view was taken in 1950, shortly before the Greencastle tram route was converted to trolleybus operation. The new wires have been erected and the new 'STOP' sign is being put in place. The tram is Moffett 307, one of a batch of 50 ordered in the early 1920s, and the ex-bus was originally 69, an AEC Regent with 52-seater Park Royal bodywork. The Corporation bought it (and others) new in 1932 to replace the assorted batch of 50 buses taken over from the private operators in 1928. It was converted to a lubricating wagon for overhead wires in March 1946 and renumbered LW 29. It was withdrawn from service on February 1953. *Robert O'Sullivan*

Above Guy 116 (FZ 7901) is passing Tower Wagon 54 (MZ 2323) in Woodstock Road (beside Beersbridge Road junction) in the early 1960s. The trolleybus is en route to Cregagh and the tower wagon crew is working on the inner pair of wires. This tower wagon was later reclassified as a 'Recovery Vehicle' after the trolleybus overhead had been dismantled in 1968, and was sold to the Corporation Electricity Department in December 1972.

The advertisement on the far wall of the shop for Persil refers to a product just as much in demand today as it was over 30 years ago. For those who would prefer to leave the washing to someone else, there was always Franklin Cleaners! *Robert Mack*

Right Although there are no trolleybuses in this photograph, I have included it because it is the only view known to me of Holywood Road in the 1950s. It was taken by Bob O'Sullivan in 1952 at the time Clough Smith were erecting the overhead for the new trolleybus service. Their tower wagon can be seen behind the car

and the partially painted traction poles have just been erected.

The bus, Daimler CWA6 209 (GZ 1877), was fitted with Harkness 56-seater bodywork when new in 1944, and was rebodied by Harkness in 1951, shortly before this photograph was taken. It was withdrawn from service in 1968, having given 24 years' service.

Although trams never operated on this part of the Holywood Road, an old-style tram stop and pole have been erected just behind the bus.

When the Holywood Road was upgraded shortly after the war, several laybys were provided at bus stops; this was fairly unusual in Belfast and several of them are still there today.

Trolleybuses operated on Holywood Road (route 25) from 24 November 1952 until 1 June 1958. At less than six years, the route was the shortest-lived in Belfast. The main reason for the early closure was the construction of the Tillysburn roundabout in connection with the Sydenham Bypass. *Robert O'Sullivan*

Tickets

During the period of trolleybus operation in Belfast there were three different ticket systems in operation.

Bell Punch System

The first system, which had operated since the days of the horse trams, was the tried and tested Bell Punch System. Essentially each fare on the system was represented by a different coloured ticket, which was pre-printed with the serial number and fare. The tickets measured about 2¼ inches by 1¼ inches. When the fare was paid, the conductor removed the appropriate ticket from the rack, inserted it into the jaws of the ticket machine and punched a single hole in the appropriate part of the ticket. The action of punching the hole sounded a bell and the machine retained the clipping. The passenger held the ticket as a receipt for the journey, as it was liable to inspection.

The machine was designed to accept only one ticket at a time and a mechanical counter registered each punch hole made. The third element in the system was the waybill. This was a record of the number of tickets sold, and cash received, at each terminus.

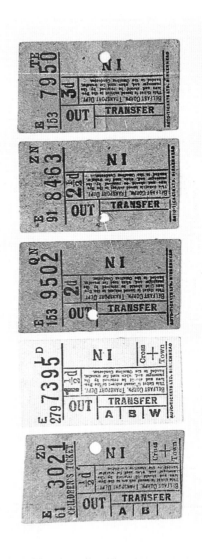

Bell Punch No 2086, together with the insignia worn by all Belfast Corporation conductors on their caps. Bus and trolleybus drivers wore the word 'Driver', while tram drivers wore the word 'Motorman'. *Mike Maybin*

A selection of Bell Punch tickets used on trolleybuses in the late 1940s and early 1950s. The serial letters are on the right above the numbers; the 'E' is the depot code, and in this case represents Haymarket trolleybus depot (for East Belfast). The 'IN' and 'OUT' refer to Castle Junction. The section on the ½d and 1d tickets marked 'Cross + Town' was used briefly on the Falls Road-Whitehouse and Carr's Glen-Cregagh services. *Mike Maybin*

The 'Ultimate' System

In the early 1950s the 'Ultimate' machine was introduced on an experimental basis. It was claimed to be much faster than the Bell Punch, although it was made by the same company. The tickets were about half the size of the Bell Punch type, but also colour-coded and pre-printed with the fare and serial number. However, the tickets were held in rolls of 500 inside the machine.

The machines were capable of recording the issue of double tickets separately, which meant that up to nine different fare values could be issued and used for later statistical analysis. Four of the mechanical counters on the front of the machine recorded only double-issue tickets, while the fifth recorded the total number of tickets issued.

Above An 'Ultimate' used in Belfast. The 'double-issue' buttons can be clearly seen under the counters. The left-hand counter recorded the total number of tickets issued and the knob on the left of the machine (or 'punch' as it was widely, if inaccurately, known) printed the stage number (00-99) on the ticket in one of three positions. Depending on the fare value these were variously 'ORD', 'CHILD', 'W. PEOPLE' or 'X TOWN'. *Mike Maybin*

Below The values of the 'Ultimate' tickets varied over the years, but initially they were 1d (blue), 1½d (white), 2d (pink), 3d (green) and 4d (primrose). The first examples had the fare pre-printed on the left, while later issues had the fare value over-printed, usually in blue. This photograph shows both types: PG 56498 (4d) was issued about 1952, while the others, IZ 00771 (3d), GT 39300 (4d) and OM 34596 (5d) were of the later over-printed variety issued about 1957. *Mike Maybin*

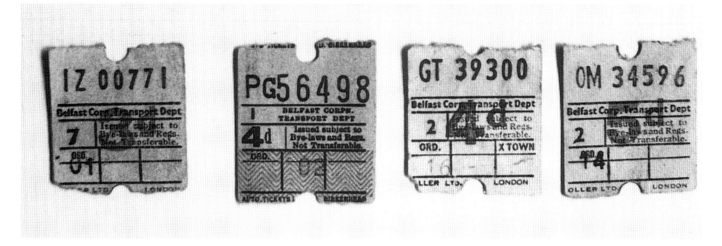

Ticket Issuing Machines (TIMs)

TIMs were introduced in the 1960s on both trolleybuses and motor buses. The two main advantages claimed over the 'Ultimates' were flexibility and cost. Twelve fares could be issued directly and recorded on separate mechanical counters, and two additional counters gave the total number of tickets issued and their total value (in halfpennies). The tickets were printed inside the machine using rolls of blank paper and therein lay the machines'

greatest drawback. The printing plates produced tickets only in halfpenny and penny denominations from ½d to 6½d. When inflation became a major problem in the late 1960s and early '70s, the cost of changing hundreds of plates was huge, and more than offset the savings achieved by substituting blank paper rolls for pre-printed tickets. However, by a clever use of multiple tickets, and the waybill, many additional fare values could be separately recorded.

Above This photograph of TIM No 618 illustrates the 'dial'-type of fare selector. The handle on the left drove the mechanism that printed the ticket, and that to the right altered the stage number printed on the ticket. While the stage number was not recorded by the machine, it was used by inspectors to check over-riding. *Mike Maybin*

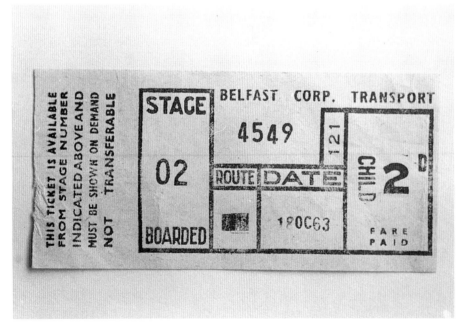

Left The ticket shown here (4549) shows the stage boarded, the fare paid, the date issued, the serial number of the ticket and the number of the machine. There was also the facility to print the route number, but this was rarely used in Belfast. *Mike Maybin*

BELFAST TROLLEYBUSES 1938-1968

Preserved trolleybuses

Five Belfast trolleybuses were identified for preservation:

98

This AEC represents the single largest class of trolleybuses in Belfast. Between 1940 and 1943 88 were delivered to allow the conversion of the East Belfast routes. No 98 (FZ 7883) was an AEC 664T with GEC electrical equipment and 68-seater Harkness bodywork. It entered service in 1943 and was retired in 1963, at which time it was prepared by Belfast Corporation to 'ex-works' standard and donated to the Ulster Folk & Transport Museum (UFTM) for preservation. Sadly, 98 was stored in the open for many years and allowed to deteriorate to the point where it is unlikely to be able to be restored.

112

No 112 (FZ 7897) represented the Guy BTX class, some 70 strong, which were delivered between 1947 and 1949, primarily to allow conversion of the North Belfast services. They were also fitted with GEC electrical equipment and Harkness bodywork to a very similar specification to the earlier AECs. This bus was also donated to the UFTM in 1968, and after lying in the open for some time has been restored to the former pristine condition in which it was received. Unlike any of the other preserved vehicles at present, 112 is in operational condition.

On 30 March 1996 112 was delivered to the Museum by the contractor who undertook the restoration, Messrs Autofit of Dungannon, and entered the new Road Gallery at Cultra under its own power. It is now on public exhibition.

168

No 168 (GZ 8532) also belonged to the Guy BTX class and was similar to 112. It was also prepared by the Corporation to 'ex-works' condition, and was donated to the National Trolleybus Association in 1968. It was stored for many years in the open, suffering considerable deterioration, although free from vandalism, and is now in private covered storage in the Midlands, its future hopefully secure. It is not available for public viewing.

183

GZ 8547 was another member of the Guy class, which again was prepared to 'ex-works' standard and donated by the Corporation to the Transport Museum Society of Ireland for preservation. It was stored in the open for many years at Castleruddery and suffered from the attention of vandals, but is now stored under cover at the Society's Museum at Howth and the hope is to restore it eventually. It is available for viewing to Museum visitors.

246

No 246 (2206 OI) was the most modern trolleybus in the Belfast fleet, entering service only in 1958. It was a four-wheel Sunbeam F4A with BTH electrical equipment and Harkness 68-seater bodywork. As with the others it was prepared to a high standard, and was donated to the London Trolleybus Preservation Society. It has been stored under cover since leaving Belfast in 1968 and has been available for public viewing at Carlton Colville near Lowestoft since 1972. It is currently being worked on and the hope is that it will be carrying visitors in 1997.

This photograph of 112 shows the excellent job of restoration carried out by Trevor Loughlin and his staff of Autofit, on behalf of the UFTM. It was taken just before the vehicle entered the Road Gallery on 30 March 1996. It is now on public display alongside the three Belfast trams. The Museum deserves great credit for commissioning this work. *Ulster Folk & Transport Museum*